Father Dave,

Thanks for everything and may you continue to live and proclaim the "Living Word."

Fr. Jerry Gard

May 30, 1965

THE PREACHING WORD

THE PREACHING WORD

On the Theology of Proclamation

OTTO SEMMELROTH S.J.

HERDER AND HERDER

1965
HERDER AND HERDER NEW YORK
232 Madison Avenue, New York 10016

Translated by John Jay Hughes.
Original edition: *Wirkendes Wort,*
Verlag Josef Knecht, Frankfurt am Main 1962.

Imprimi potest: Friedr. Buuck S.J.
Praep. Prov. Germ. Inf.

Nihil obstat: Patrick A. Barry
Censor Librorum

Imprimatur: Patrick C. Brennan
Vicar General, Diocese of Burlington
October 19, 1964

The nihil obstat and imprimatur are official declarations that a book or pamphlet is free of doctrinal or moral error. No implication is contained therein that those who have granted the nihil obstat and imprimatur agree with the contents, opinions or statements expressed.

Library of Congress Catalog Card Number: 64–19737

Printed in the United States of America

Contents

Translator's Note

We have in English two ways of differentiating "the inspired word of God in holy scripture" from "the Word became flesh and dwelt among us." In the former case "word" is uncapitalized and is referred to by the pronouns it and which. But when "word" is used to refer to the Logos, the second person of the Trinity, it is capitalized and must be referred to by the pronouns "he" and "who": to refer to the "Word" (Logos) as "it" would be at the least a gross theological error, and at worst heresy.

German however knows no such distinction: first, because every noun in German is capitalized, and second because "word" ("Wort") is grammatically neuter and must always be referred to by the neuter pronoun, even when it designates the second person of the Trinity. It is, therefore, obviously impossible in the original German version of this book to decide in every case and beyond all shadow of doubt whether the author is talking about the word or about the Word—in fact, it is clear that he not infrequently means both, or that he deliberately leaves the question open in order to bring out his views about the analogous use of the term "word." To have attempted, therefore, to decide each time whether it should be "word" or "Word" in English would have amounted to an interpretation of the author's thought beyond the competence of the translator, whose job is to render the original faithfully, clearly and readably, without intruding his own ideas or interpretation. Hence the term "word" has been left uncapitalized throughout, save for those rare cases when the context made it impossible to avoid capitalization. This is also, of course, the reason why readers will occasionally find our Lord ("the Word") apparently referred to as "it" or "which."

JOHN JAY HUGHES

Augustinianum, Gaesdonck bei Goch

Introduction

In the evangelists' report of the miraculous draught of fishes this event is interpreted as affording a program for the vocation of the apostles to be catchers of men. We shall not go wrong if we interpret Simon Peter's words (in Lk 5:5) in the same way, as presenting a program for the Christian life: "Master, we have toiled all night and taken nothing! Nevertheless, at your word I will let down the nets." Three important assertions about the word of God are made here. First is the tacit assumption that the Christian life is determined by the impact of God's word. And then this word proves to be in no way limited to the mere communication of facts. It is a challenge to action, though to be sure the action demanded proceeds from what the word has made known. Finally, human life is transformed precisely through the impact of this word of God. Man's practical reason arrives at conclusions and decisions; and these are transcended by the revelations and demands of God's word. Even if we maintain with Catholic teaching that God's word does not invalidate the correct insights and expectations of human reason, but rather fulfills and elevates them, it is still true that God's word challenges a man's actual plans and his behavior, causing him to correct and even reverse them. Therefore the basic attitude of him who has been called and redeemed by Christ is summarized in the motto: "Nevertheless, at your word . . ."

For this reason an interpretation of God's word is of

fundamental importance for the Christian's understanding of his calling. Interpretation means here not merely explaining the contents of the individual utterances of God's word —that this is of great importance is self-evident. But at least as necessary and difficult is the task of explaining what exactly the word of God is, where it seeks to impart itself to him who listens for it, and in what manner it strives to exert in him its divine power and force.

The word of God is wrapped obscurely in the veil of mystery. This is stated with emphasis in the last book of holy scripture. "He has a name inscribed which no one knows by himself. . . . And the name by which he is called is The Word of God" (Ap 19:12f). No matter how deep therefore our obligation to investigate painstakingly the word of God and its power, we must respect this mystery. What our Lord has said about the mystery of his Father applies here in analogous form: "No one knows the Father but the Son and him to whom the Son chooses to reveal him" (Mt 11:27).

Thus any attempt to interpret theologically the word of God and its proclamation in the church must be done in the spirit of him who listens: it must preserve the character of meditation. From the purely "scholarly" point of view a number of things which will be said here could perhaps be left unsaid. Meditative listening—even though imbued with the necessary caution and reserve—will again and again reach out beyond the bounds of scholarship and attempt through living perception and discernment to trace lines which are not sufficiently certain to be adopted by scholarship.

OTTO SEMMELROTH

PART ONE

THE REALITY OF GOD'S WORD

If we wish to speak of the word of God in the church and especially of the significance of God's word as portrayed in the church for salvation and of its power of imparting grace, we are faced with a considerable difficulty. For it is not at all clear just what the word of God means. We can hardly doubt that this concept denotes one way in which the invisible God makes himself known to men—perhaps every way in which he does so. After all, the concept "word" should not lose its original meaning completely when it is employed for God's communication of himself. But one need cast no more than a cursory glance at holy scripture and listen but briefly to the manner in which the church gives utterance to its life of faith to notice that there are obviously very many different ways in which God has communicated himself to men. All these ways are called from time to time the word of God. Moreover if one ascribes to the word of God creative efficacy and the imparting of grace, a clear distinction of the concept "word of God" is seen to be very necessary. For even if one ventures to claim that divine grace is imparted at all by the proclamation of God's word, one would certainly not dare to maintain that all the different ways in which the word has been uttered or proclaimed are equally effective communications of grace. The question of the efficacious impartation of grace is not an either-or proposition; rather it can have very different degrees of intensity. And these differences may very well vary in accordance with the degree in which a given divine communication can really be called a word of God.

Here we come up against a boundary which is placed upon the efforts of theologians of all ages, and which has never left them in peace. Again and again they are tempted illicitly to overstep the boundaries of their tasks. This limitation makes it necessary to speak in analogies, a necessity of which scholarship is not at all enamoured. Scholarship has the ambition of determining and delineating in its statements the object of its study with as much precision and as little ambiguity as possible. Theologians have not always taken sufficient note of the fact that the general estimation which has tipped the scales in favor of the "exact" sciences does not justify the adoption of new methods which the nature of their own science can by no means support. Theology has therefore not infrequently become untrue to its own nature and to its tasks by trying to obscure the difference between its own kind of scholarship and that of the exact sciences. All too often it seems as if theology wants to be an exact science too. For this reason theology is no longer fond of analogy, although analogy belongs to theology's very essence. But precisely in treating the word of God in the church it is important to remain aware of the various ways in which this word is manifested and therefore of the analogous character of the concept itself. Otherwise we fail to appreciate the divine power which in certain cases the proclamation of God's word has, for this mysterious power is not always present when the word of God is manifested. Or else we fall into the temptation of ascribing to every utterance of God's word this imparting of grace which one can and must assert in those cases where the word of God is realized with special intensity. And either of these courses would be an improper generalization. For the assertion that the word of God, in distinction from the sacraments, is always without any efficacy for the imparting of grace is just as unacceptable as the assertion that, wherever we find mention of the word of God, we are confronted with a mystery in which God imparts himself and his grace fully and unequivocally. "We speak mostly very rashly of 'truth' or of 'the word of God,' summarizing under each of these notions quite different kinds of things. Thus we create a source of much unclarity and even of occasions for the division of Christendom."[1]

Our first task is, therefore, to stake out various areas in which the notion of God's word is employed. The boundaries separating these areas from one another confront us with a double task. In the first place we must take them seriously, observing them as genuine lines of separation. That is to say, we must guard ourselves against seeing an equivalent manifestation of God's word without distinction in the various areas, simply because the phrase "word of God" is employed in each case. But on the other hand it belongs to the analogous use of notions with the same name that their delimitation should not create a chasm between them too large to be bridged. Therefore the use of the notion of God's word cannot be totally different in one area from its use in another. There must be a *fundamentum in re,* an inherent reason for speaking of the word of God in each case. Thus both the distinction and the common core of meaning must be worked out.

We shall investigate in the three sections of this book the three areas in which the word of God is manifested. Although it is in the terminology of revelation not the original or primary way of speaking of God's word, we shall, for reasons having to do with the systematic presentation of objective reality, take as the first area the word of God within the Godhead itself. Secondly we shall consider the area in which, so to speak, God steps creatively outside of himself, and thus into that area in which he has also uttered his word. And in this area in which God utters his word we must consider especially the actual area governed by listening to the word of God, namely the church. For after all, in the type of the Lord's mother the church is described as the community of those who hear the word of God and heed it (Lk 8:21).

1 The Word of God within the Godhead

1 In the Beginning Was the Word

The mysterious prologue of the fourth gospel has always troubled the spirit of man. Goethe was not the first to cause his Faust to mutter over this word. The temptation to put work before the word and to proclaim as a higher gospel "In the beginning was the deed" has never let go of man. It is typical of our activistic age that it ascribes greater importance to action than to the spoken or pondered word in our lives, typical too that philosophy proclaims the priority of activity over thought and the word whereby thought is expressed. But the evangelical preaching remains unchanged: in the beginning was the word.

The Word as a Reality in the Economy of Redemption

The contrary temptation may also arise within the context of Christian faith and its theological exercise. One can be so determined to conceive of the primal word in terms of its existence at the heart of the Godhead that one does not see the foreground, namely the earthly reality, which is after all of primary importance here.

In order to interpret properly the word that John says was in the beginning we must follow the path marked out by the New Testament, and indeed within the New Testament by

John himself, if we are to realize what this word really is. The thought of John's prologue of course reaches back into that eternity in which Jesus Christ, who is the heart and principal subject of the johannine gospel, existed and lived before he was, in the incarnation, uttered into the world as the word of his Father. We might be tempted therefore to rest all too snugly in this concept when speaking of the word of the Father within the Godhead, the word who is Jesus Christ from all eternity. But we dare not overlook the fact that this concept of the divine word in a mode of existence without beginning and without end is not John's essential meaning when he speaks of the incarnate son of God as God's word. Christ could be called the word in the prologue of John's gospel because and insofar as he has in the incarnation assumed a mode of existence which is, in relation to the God who speaks, exterior. This is the distinguishing feature of the spoken word, that it is exterior to the speaker. But the incarnate word of God is not, as are the words men speak, removed from the control of him who utters this word once he has spoken it. The word of God uttered in the incarnation is and remains God himself, the speaker of this word.

The visible and tangible humanity of our Lord has its being in the inviolable person of the Son of God. Thus all man's efforts to silence this word are in vain. Men cannot suppress its sound and urgency by removing Christ from humanity's reverent recognition through crucifixion, or from sight and hearing through burial in the grave. But this word of God which has been communicated once and for all is risen no more to die. As the resounding word of God, and therefore as visible and audible, this word continues to live in the church. And although in the church this word is exposed to the grasp and oppression of those who will not hear it, yet it can never be totally silenced.

The primary and immediate meaning of the word of God in John's prologue is the utterance of the second divine person in his efficacious role within the economy of redemption.[2] This meaning complements the observation we make of the New Testament in general. Evidence for the doctrine of the Trinity can certainly be found in the pages of the New Testament. But the Trinity appears in the New Testament not so much doctrinally—as a statement about the nature of the Godhead—but rather "economically." That is to say, Father, Son and Holy Ghost appear as dividing and sharing the work of redemption between them.

In antiquity this observation was cited in an attempt to justify modalism, the erroneous teaching that the three persons were three modes in which the one God in his single person appeared and worked. "The Trinity is not spoken of speculatively in the New Testament, but rather insofar as it has taken on the form of our existence; or, vice versa, our existence is treated insofar as it has become trinitarian, insofar as it is, in the Spirit, through Christ, on the way to the Father. This means that the scriptures' proclamation of the Trinity comes about from the historical person of Jesus Christ and from the historical fact of the pouring out of the Holy Spirit."[3]

Apart from the New Testament texts which distribute God's activity within the economy of redemption among three subjects, these three persons stand out quite clearly as equal persons within the Godhead having the same substance. This is made clear above all by the trinitarian formulas (e.g. Mt 28:19; Lk 24:49; Jn 14:16f; Acts 2:32f; Rom 5:1–5; 1 Cor 2:6–16; 2 Cor 1:21f; Gal 4:4f; Eph 1:3–14; 2 Th 2:13; Tit 3:4–11; Heb 2:2f; 1 Pt 1:1f; 1 Jn 3:23f; Jude 20f).

Nonetheless it is understandable that, since the threefold character of the one God does not appear in the New

Testament in the form of a doctrinal synthesis, the church in its first general councils (Nicea in 325 and Constantinople in 381) felt called upon to specify that the Son and the Holy Spirit are of the same substance with the Father. "The characteristic peculiarity of the New Testament consists precisely in its tacit and, in the last analysis, absolutely definite refusal to explain rationally the threefold nature of the one God in terms of a mere appearance and 'aspect adopted for our sakes' or, on the other hand . . . to make this threefold nature understandable by making the Son and the Spirit either mythical beings of an intermediate kind or in a more intensely religious way by making them something 'human.' "[4] This "economic" Trinity—the Trinity in action—is grounded rather in the immanent and genuine threefold nature of the persons within the Godhead itself.

The Word within the Godhead

What has been said applies also to the designation of the incarnate Son of God as the word of God in which God communicates himself. Here again we have an utterance that applies first of all within the economy of redemption: Christ is God's communication of himself into the world he has created. But this redemptive utterance is founded in the nature of the incarnate Christ as he exists in the Godhead. Augustine was probably the first Christian thinker who specifically referred the johannine "word" back to the nature of the second person of the trinitarian God as he exists within the Godhead. And it was due to his so-called psychological portrayal of the divine Trinity that this concept came to be the common possession at least of the western church.[5] It is true that the apologists of Christian antiquity had already employed the stoic's distinction between the interior and the exterior word. But Augustine was perhaps the first to employ this distinction extensively, applying it to the twofold manner in which Christ is the word; for Augustine attempts to explain the relationship of the Father and Logos within the Godhead on the basis of a human metaphor. Or more precisely, Augustine distinguishes in human speech a threefold word. Before speaking his word externally the speaker must first form a concept of the word. These two kinds of word, the exterior utterance and its internal conception, vary according to the language a man uses to express himself, be it Greek or Latin or Punic. But underlying both forms of the word is the interior word, the thought, the notional word, which must be conceived before it can be exteriorly uttered in any given language. And this conceptual, intellectual word is not bound by any difference in language.[6] It is this interior word in the thinking mind of the speaker—who has of course been created in the image of God—that Augustine uses to provide an idea of the second person of the Trinity. "What is that word which is spoken and passes not away? There is, even in man himself, a word which remains within; for only the echo comes forth from the mouth. There is a word which is in truth intellectually spoken."[7]

The human mind, in reflecting upon itself, utters its recognition in the conceptual word "I" and thus in a certain sense stands face to face with itself. This is a suitable image of what happens in the threefold God when the Father recognizes himself and utters himself in the Son. This image is of course limited, a factor we must take into account if we are to avoid drawing conclusions contrary to faith. But the justification of this image is the creation of man according to the image and likeness of God. The Father does not recognize himself unless he places himself face to face with the contents of this self-recognition in the form of a "conceptual word." And this conceptual word which confronts him is the Son. This is also the precise reason why the Son came to us in the incarnation as the image of the invisible God (Col 1:15), because he is already in the interior life of the Godhead the image, the mirror and the spiritual word of the Father as the Father recognizes himself. And just for this reason too is the incarnation a self-utterance of God to men, the self-utterance of a God whose word is the incarnate one. All who receive this word in faith and hear this word are given by the word the power to become children of God. For this word, a word uttered exteriorly, was also in the beginning, and was God himself (Jn 1:1); so that he who hears this word is taken up in grace into the interior life of God.

Thus Jesus Christ is not only the word of God who comes into the world he has created: he came unto his own. And of course the world is his own precisely because "all things came into being through him, and without him there came to be not one thing that has come to be" (Jn 1:3). For the Father, in uttering his self-recognition within the Godhead in the Son, sees and utters at the same time the possibility and the reality of the world which is to be created. Thus, long before God gave the world a real existence in time, he has uttered this world in his eternal conceptual word, the Son, and has given it in this way a reality within the Godhead. "The Father utters himself and all creatures in the word which he begets, inasmuch as the begotten word is an adequate representation of the Father and of all creatures."[8] The Son is also the word within the Godhead in which not only God's own essence but also the essence and reality of the creation is recognized and uttered.

2 The Word of God as Analogous Reality

We have in religious thought and in theology become quite accustomed to speaking of Christ as the word of God whenever we wish to refer to his existence within the

Trinity. That he is, within the Godhead, the word in which the Father utters himself is the basis for the further fact that he is the self-communication of the invisible God to man, who is bound to the body and therefore to a revelation which can be apprehended sensibly.

Utterance within the Godhead as the Root of the Incarnation

Objectively considered, this line of thought is certainly not erroneous. As a matter of fact there is an intrinsic reason why precisely the second person of the triune God became man, and not the Father or the Holy Spirit. For the incarnation is very like a translation of the Son's existence within the Godhead into the world of creatures. It was not by an arbitrary decree of God that the Son and none other became man. The incarnation could not without alteration of its significance have occurred in a different way. If it is true that the Son is, in the inner life of the Godhead, the interior word, the thought, the concept in which the Father perceives himself, and if the incarnation is the commencement of the atoning dialog between God and man, then it is in harmony with the divine logic that he who within the Godhead is the word should become man and by so doing become the word outside the Godhead, the word perceptible to man. (And in this connection it should be noted that this dialog, as we have termed it, is carried out not merely in words which we must recognize and in admonitions which we must follow, but in revelations and deeds of great power through which God himself becomes part of our history, and thereby himself shapes this history.) Thus it is in accord with the objective truth of things as they actually are to state that the second divine person is from all eternity the Father's expression of himself, and that his mission to us men as the word is the divine consequence of this eternal truth.

The case however is different when we ask which of these two truths is immediately and primarily denoted by the concept "word of God." Here the order should probably be reversed: we should take "word" as designating primarily the going forth of the Son into the world outside the Godhead. The procession of the Son from the Father within the Godhead, on the other hand, has only a secondary claim to the title "word"—that is, as the foundation for the Son's procession into the outside world. The designation of the second divine person in his relation to the first is not what is primarily meant when Jesus Christ is described as the word of God. In the case of human speech we mean primarily by the term "word" the word which is uttered outwardly and which creates a bond with others. And it is only secondarily that we mean by "word" the thought which a man has conceived before he gives it audible expression in words. And the case is similar with regard to the divine utterance through Jesus Christ and his eternal existence with the Godhead.

A word means first of all the expression in which a speaker reveals and communicates what is within him. "Do you not know that everything which is uttered in an intelligible voice with any kind of meaning is called a word?"[9] And Augustine applies this definition in another passage to the word of the Father: Christ "is called the word of the Father because through him the Father is known. Thus just as we manage through our words, when we speak the truth, to make our minds known to the hearer and to reveal to another through such signs what we carry secretly in our hearts, so is it entirely fitting that the wisdom begotten of God the Father should be termed his word, because through this wisdom the inscrutable Father is made known to deserving souls."[10] We are indebted to Augustine for applying the concept "word" to the word within the Godhead, the second person of the Trinity. And even he does not overlook the fact that to reveal is the special characteristic of the word. But then the word must be actually present when it is spoken to a listener if it is to communicate to him the hidden interior of the speaker. The speculative Logos-theology of the Greek fathers was aware of this. "Just as the human Logos reveals the mind of man from whom this Logos proceeds, so does the Son-Logos reveal the mind of the Father from whom the Logos is begotten. It is of the essence of the Logos to be the revealer of the Father."[11]

Today it can hardly be doubted that the "word" of the prologue to John's gospel denotes the divine person who proceeds from the Father in eternal preexistence as the Father's expression of himself. But it is also generally recognized that John called this divine person the word because and insofar as he has become man and has thus been communicated to men as the word of God. It is true that scholars have not been able to clarify completely the question of the origin of the stimuli which impelled John, or the primitive Christian authors of the Logos hymn at the beginning of the johannine gospel, to represent Jesus' significance in the drama of redemption with this Logos conception. Among the various explanations however only one, and that the most unlikely, would argue that the Logos does not primarily denote an utterance and a communication. This theory contends that the johannine concept of Logos is derived from the hellenistic and stoic speculation about the Logos as cosmic idea. All other possible sources of the johannine concept of Logos—Judeo-Christian thought, the Old Testament theology of the word of God, the hellenistic conception of the Logos as found for instance in Philo, or finally pre-Christian gnosticism—all these consider Logos to mean an intermediate being between God and the world, a being joining the two with each other. Thus in any case the Logos represents an utterance of God to the world, a word spoken by him in order to communicate himself. This word achieved its fullest reality in Christ, since he who is from eternity the "thought" of the Father became in the incarnation the word uttered by the Father to the world.

This conclusion does not deny, indeed it assumes that the reason for understanding the incarnation of the Son as the utterance of God's word is that from eternity the Father recognizes himself in the Son and utters himself in him. Thus it is possible for John to link this word, which he describes as exercising perfectly in the incarnation the function of the word to man, with the preexistent reality of the Son as well, in his capacity as the eternal thought of the Father.

In both cases the concept "word" is employed analogously. The dissimilarity between the two ways the term is employed results from the fact that the word is actually intended to denote an utterance. In this sense the concept finds its full realization in the incarnation. But in an extended sense "word" is also applied to the interior concept which forms the foundation for the utterance. And this latter sense applies to the Son as he exists within the Godhead. For there is the root and substance of that which in the incarnation comes forth in the form of the uttered word.

Procession and Mission

The connection between the word uttered in the incarnation and the roots of this word within the Godhead should be compared not merely with the connection between men's concepts and the words in which they express them. The word within the Godhead is not only the root of the word expressed exteriorly: the word's procession from the Father is also the pattern for the sending forth of the word in the incarnation. It is not merely that the uttered word communicates in substance the contents of what has previously, within the Godhead, been conceived by the mind of God. The empirical advent of God's word in the incarnation which takes place in virtue of the divine sending is the image of a genuine procession of the "conceptual word" within the Godhead, originating with the person of the Father who has conceived it and who, therefore, confronts it as well. Although the eternal word of God, the second person of the triune God, is not only of the same substance with the first person but also is the first person inwardly, the second person is still distinct from the first and confronts him in a genuine sense. Insofar as the Father in his self-recognition confronts his image, so to speak, we can in fact say that the procession of the second person from the first is also an "utterance," even though this is not actually the case.

Thus the description of the second person in God as the word is justified not only because the word within the Godhead is in substance the root for the exteriorly communicated word of revelation, but in the further fact that the Father utters and communicates himself within the Godhead in the generation of the Son; and in so doing he provides an image of all free communication and revelation outside the Godhead.

Augustine found in several scriptural texts the observation that in human speech the word uttered externally is preceded by an internal word that came to be embodied in the spoken word. He discovered biblical texts in which thought is distinguished from the utterance of the thought, in which therefore an interior word is given priority over the exterior word. Wisdom 2:1 reads: "They said to themselves, reasoning unsoundly . . ." And Matthew reports: "The scribes said to themselves, 'He is blaspheming.' " That this interior speech is a thought, the substance of which is uttered, is shown by Christ's question which follows: "Why do you think evil in your hearts?" (Mt 9:4). "They began to think, saying . . ." (Lk 5:21f).[12]

So the second divine person is really the word within the Godhead. But this use of the concept "word" is still analogous. We use "word" in its immediate and actual sense to denote those cases where something is communicated to a person who is external to the speaker. The word communicates to this person something hitherto secret and private to the speaker in order that this communication may be accepted. But it could also be refused.

2 God's Word Without

It has probably become clear that there is enough similarity between the "word character" of the second divine person within the Godhead and the word of God sent forth to men in the incarnation for us to be able to call them both God's word. But it should be equally clear that they are sufficiently different to raise the question which of these two modes of existence has prior claim to the term "word." This question must not be answered too lightly. If we look for what is prior in essence, that on which the other is founded, then we must unquestionably grant priority to the word within the Godhead. If however we inquire about the immediate sense of word then we must point to the external word. For, since the actual sense of word is the communication of what is hidden within, the word is realized precisely at the point at which it has left the interior of the thinker and has through speech outwardly come to the notice of others. The word is something peculiar to the social life of man. In the inner life of the Godhead, and also in the intercourse of angels, no actual word is necessary. It is only by analogy that we can speak of the word as existing among men and in the Godhead.

But even in cases where a man's word comes to another man, or where God's word comes to us men, we are not always speaking of word in the same way. And here too the concept "word" is analogous, that is, despite great similarities in meanings the term is employed in different ways.

Especially in God's revelation of himself to man in his word does the term have a diverse meaning, one which, despite all affinity, is nevertheless distinct. If we truly wish in some measure to realize what the coming of God's word means for us, how it is meant to be effective in us and how we should receive this word, then we must investigate carefully the significance of God's word in each individual case. For the answering word is governed always by the original utterance. And we can receive a word only when we know how it can be heard.

The difficulty here is that words are never alone. The word always appears linked with something else. Thus it comes about that we expand "word" from its strict significance to denote what is linked with it as well. We will investigate therefore how God's word is linked with his revelation, his work, and with the human word of answer.

1 Word and Revelation

What the concept of God's word is most closely linked with, what indeed it seems at first to be identical with, is his revelation. Theological tradition continues to maintain that the word of God has a revealing function even when focusing its attention on the immanent existence of the second person of the triune God within the Godhead and assigning to him the title "word." And the manner whereby the nature of divine revelation and its issuance is presented in fundamental theology not infrequently leaves the impression that revelation and God's word are equated.

The Connection between God's Word and His Revelation

Fundamental theology is correct in its definition of revelation as "God's word of testimony." There is today considerable resistance to this definition, a resistance arising from the fear that the notion of revelation will become too intellectualized if it is confined to God's utterance—in distinction to his acts. And it must be admitted that the intellectualizing danger is by no means banished merely by emphasizing that God also reveals himself in his acts. Rather we must come to understand God's utterance not only as the communication of new insights, but also as the conveying of a genuine self-giving from person to person. This occurs among men, for instance, when a speaker conveys what is in his mind to the person whom he is addressing; words are the necessary means of expression for such communication. This fact cannot be overlooked or denied, despite the need for caution with regard to intellectualism. It is certainly true that God's revelatory speech is always embedded in acts. But revelation as such, that is to say, as the drawing aside of the veil of secrecy, comes about first of all through the communication of a certain idea to man's faculty of comprehension. This idea must then be accepted by the intellect if it is to obtain response and decision from the will and thereby determine the course of life. In other words in the total process whereby God communicates himself to man the formal revelatory element is precisely utterance, a knocking on the door of a man's perceptive faculties in order to communicate an idea.

Once we have this process the identification of God's word with revelation is not too difficult. It seems as if we could just as well say "the word of God goes forth" as "his revelation goes forth." Did not the prophets, in communicating God's word to their people—whether it be revelation of God's mysteries or warning and challenge—introduce their proclamation with the formulas "The word of the Lord, thus saith the Lord"? Did they not begin their proclamation with the incisive warning: "And now hear, O Jacob, my servant, and Israel whom I have chosen" (Is 44:1)? Hearing is of course primarily the reception of the word spoken by another. But hearing is also the acceptance of divine revelation in faith. Faith comes from hearing (Rom 10:17). Thus revelation and God's word appear to be identical.

In common usage we do very often simply identify the two. The Council of Trent, in saying that "this truth and discipline is contained in written books and in unwritten traditions," means by "truth and discipline" "the gospel which was once promised by the prophets in the holy scriptures, which our Lord, Jesus Christ, the Son of God, first proclaimed with his own mouth, and which he then commanded to be preached by his apostles to every creature as the source of all saving truth and moral discipline."[13] The truth contained in scripture and in tradition is, therefore, God's revelation. But at the same time we say that scripture and tradition contain God's word. Thus revelation and word seem once again to be identified. However the attentive observer may notice that precisely here a noteworthy distinction presses itself upon his consciousness. Scripture and tradition do not have the same relationship to God's word. In substance they both contain God's word, so to speak, the word that God has spoken. But holy scripture does not merely contain God's word: as an inspired book it *is* his word. For scripture has God for its author,[14] and this cannot be said of tradition.

In defining the church's task of proclamation however we generally identify revelation and the word of God without giving the matter any special thought. The church stands in the service of God's word. Therefore it is God's word which the church proclaims. But we are equally convinced that the church's task of proclamation is to make known God's revelation. This revelation Jesus Christ issued once for all to his apostles, it was issued by them to the church, and this same revelation the church must again and again proclaim and interpret to men. So that if we want to say what it is that the church has to proclaim, it seems that we can mention interchangeably either God's word or his revelation.

The Difference between Revelation and God's Word

We shall have to look much more closely at these two so closely related things, God's revelation and his word, to ascertain the difference between them. But because this distinction is not perceptible to the superficial observer, the whole question of the relationship between God's word and his revelation can give the impression of hair-splitting that has no great importance for lively faith in God's word and revelation. It is, after all, the content of what God has revealed which man must accept in faith. And that this content is received because God testifies to its truth is what gives to man's encounter with God in faith its power to save. But the question whether this encounter is called acceptance of revelation or hearing the word does not seem at present to be of any too great importance. To be sure, only in the later course of our presentation will this distinction achieve its full importance. If we wish to ascertain just where God's word is to be found in the church, and more especially if we must show how God's word can be present in the church without there being any further divine revelation, it is quite important to have made a distinction between God's word and his revelation.

This distinction between God's revelation and his word becomes perceptible in the manner whereby we speak of them. The revelation of any person, and therefore God's revelation, occurs through speech. Such speech need not always take place in an utterance formed by the lips and in sentences. It can also occur through other signs which man uses—either with his limbs or with the help of outside things that can help him express what was previously closeted inside his person. Applied to God, this means that speech does not have to consist of audible words between God and men. It can also be communicated to the perceiving mind of man without any bodily expression, in such a way that man recognizes the substance of what is uttered. When speech is used to express something that lies in that guarded, secret area of a person then such speech also has the character of a gift, for it occurs as the result of the free decision of the person making the revelation, and whose distinguishing characteristic is that he can remain shut up in himself if he does not wish to reveal himself and thereby lay himself open.

But is such speech the same thing as the word? Certainly revelation occurs in word, just as revelation occurs in speech. Nevertheless speech and word are not the same. For if we ask what it is that is spoken, the answer is that the word is spoken. The word is thus the object of speech. It is not identical with speech.

Is then the word the content of speech, of revelation? We might suppose so from the fact that the word is the object of speech, and that we also call the content communicated in speech its object. And yet the content of revelation is not identical with the word through which revelation is uttered. We receive the revealed content in the word, because the word is that vessel and means through which the content of speech is conveyed to the hearer. So the word is the means of speech and of revealing. It is not however a causative means, an instrument employed in order to produce, physically, with its help, an effect. Rather, in the manner of a concrete vessel, it is a means of expression which contains speech's content, and it conveys this content to the hearer. Between the vessel of the word and the content which it communicates there exist, to be sure, a connection and a solidarity so close that the hearer has at times some trouble unwrapping the intellectual content and separating it from the verbal vessel containing it. Precisely because of this close and living solidarity we are tempted again and again to identify word and speech, the verbal vessel and the content it communicates, the means of expression and the goal of communication.

The distinction between word and revelation becomes still clearer if we consider just how it is that revelation occurs. This is certainly a mysterious process in the depths of a human being, a mystery even to him, and all the more so for all others. But just because it is so difficult to grasp in concrete expression the deepest center of a human being to whom God's revelation is made, so should we be warned against attempting to simplify the matter by conceiving of the issuance of divine revelation to man on the model of man's speech to man. A human being, unlike God, who is pure spirit, can never communicate himself directly to another. A man must always try first to put his innermost secrets into concrete form if he wishes to communicate them to a fellow man. Indeed, before he can reveal them he must try, often with great difficulty, consciously to recognize what is there in the depths of his being. Hence this self-discovery is itself always a form of expression. And this is the limit placed on our communication of ourselves. We can never communicate what is in us entirely as it is; in being objectized it inevitably loses something of its actual form.

But when God communicates himself in revelation he is able to penetrate immediately and subjectively to the innermost depths of a human being and make himself knowable to him. By means of this penetration into its depths, the soul attains knowledge of God in a fullness quite impossible for man without such communication. Such knowledge brings to him who is granted it the unshakable certainty that this communication comes from God himself. He also receives what God communicates of himself clearly and luminously, without there being any word to serve as the vessel containing the communication. This was the immediate knowledge of God which the prophets had when God spoke to them. This is what happens when God speaks through the Holy Spirit to the apostles in the New Testament. And this occurs as well when God makes himself knowable and communicates himself to individuals in post-apostolic times in a genuine mystical experience.

When the person who encounters God directly in this way emerges from the experience the substance of the revelation made to him is supposed to live on in him and continue to exercise its influence on him. The experience is given to him not merely for the moment of his charismatic encounter with God, but for his entire life. Moreover this revelation is intended not for him alone, but for them also to whom he is sent. This is even true with regard to private revelations, which even in the post-apostolic time continue to occur, and which are joined with the command to work for the salvation of others.

In the case of a public revelation which an individual hears direct from God, the proclamation of the message to men is in fact the primary and the real reason for God's communication to his prophet. But this means that something which has been received inwardly and subjectively must be expressed outwardly and objectively. This is essential simply in order that what the recipient has received may continue to live on later when he is no longer under the influence of the event in which God reveals himself, but when at the same time he must still live from this revelation. And the expression of the message in outward and objective form is even more necessary in order that God's revelation of himself may be publicly passed on to the people of God. The substance of the revelation can be passed on only in the vessel of the word, through the words coined for this purpose: it must be made audible by human means. It may happen that the recipient of the revelation has already been given the verbal formula of expression along with the revelation itself. But we know from the testimony of those chosen men who have been singled out to be the recipients of divine revelation how terribly difficult it often is for them to pass on what they have learned of God. No human words, no matter how skillfully formulated and arranged, seem to be able to express the experience they have had of the divine reality. Their difficulty is twofold. It comes first of all from the agonizing discovery of how little prepared men are to receive God's supernatural power and efficacy. "Who has believed our report? And to whom has the arm of the Lord been revealed?" (Is 53:1). "I have been very jealous for the Lord, the God of hosts; for the people of Israel have forsaken your covenant, thrown down your altars, and slain your prophets with the sword" (1 Chr 19:14). But the prophets' difficulty proceeds also from the agonizing discrepancy between the mission they have received to proclaim God's revelation and the insufficiency of the human words which must serve as the vessel to contain this revelation. "Ah, Lord God! Behold, I do not know how to speak . . ." (Jer 1:6): thus does the prophet Jeremiah seek to escape God's call which sends him forth to pass on the words of God's revelation. "But the Lord put forth his hand and touched my mouth; and the Lord said to me, 'Behold, I put my words in your mouth' " (Jer 1:9). God also assists the bearer of his revelation by providing him with some suitable means for transmitting what he has learned.

All this shows that God's word and his revelation are not

simply identical. The word of God is his revelation; but it is his revelation expressed and made objective, having its roots in the event of revelation and perhaps even formed by this event, but nonetheless transcending the event by expressing it.

Thus we receive God's revelation in his word in very much the same way as we meet the second person of the triune God in Jesus, the man of flesh and blood. Jesus, the man with a human body, is God. And yet, when we look at Jesus Christ as he walked once upon the earth, we do not see God with the same directness as in the heavenly vision, a vision "immediate, without the mediation of any creature which is itself in any way the object of this vision."[15] So God's word is the bodily and human form expressing that divine content we truly meet in this word. And yet the word is different from the direct recipient of God's revelation, even though it contains this revelation. Actually the word is always the subsequent objective wrapping in which the human recipient of revelation must veil his unveiled experience of revelation—for himself and all the more for others. In this way he, as well as other men, can receive again and again in this dress that which God has communicated. Moreover he can bring it alive again in that fundamental act of the Christian life we call faith.

2 God's Word and His Work

The related notions of word and revelation which we have treated above lead us at once to a further connection in which God's word very frequently appears. Precisely because God's word proves to be a means for the expression of revelation, and a vessel containing revelation, we must compare this word with another kind of vessel and means of expression whereby divine revelation also comes to us.

Revelation occurs not only in word but also through God's work. Through the things he does God ceases to be distant and comes near to us. And so we must investigate the relationship and distinction between word and work, so that we may understand more precisely the nature of God's word from this point of view as well.

The Connection between God's Word and His Work

We cannot simply separate God's word and his work, if only because God, in speaking, is at work. Speech is always a kind of action. Therefore the spoken (or written) word is also the result of an action, and therefore work. This is of course the reason why it is also possible to call the God-man the word of the Father, and to confront him with the Father who is the speaker of the Logos—and why, on the other hand, it is then necessary to investigate more closely this attribution of the word to the Father alone. Insofar as Christ is God's creative self-proclamation, and in this sense the word of God, it is only by appropriation that we can term him the word of the *Father*. For what God effects outside of his triune inner life is not the work of one of the three divine persons, but has its roots in God's threefold unity. Thus when it is ascribed to one of the three persons this is done not in the sense of something which belongs to that person exclusively (*proprium*), but rather as a purely intellectual appropriation. Therefore to the extent that God's word is considered an act performed by God as speaker, the work is always the word of the three persons taken together. But inasmuch as God's word exists once and for all and communicates something through its content, it is referred to each of the three divine persons in a particular manner. Because the word God speaks is the image of the personal word spoken by the Father within the Godhead, and as such the bearer of this personal word's substance, its relationship to the Son is different from its relationship to the Father and to the Holy Spirit. This observation—which may at first sight seem somewhat like hair-splitting—should be made here merely to confirm the fact that God's word is, when uttered, always a work as well. And it is subject therefore, like all the works of God, to the principle defined by the Council of Florence that "Father, Son and Holy Spirit are not three sources of creation, but one source."[16] And the word, insofar as it comes into being, is "created" and thus has as its source not the Father alone, but Father, Son and Holy Spirit.

But the word of God is related to his work not merely to the extent that it is the result of a divine action. The word of God also possesses the character of work inasmuch as its promulgation has an effect on the man to whom it is communicated. "The word of God is living and active, sharper than any two-edged sword" (Heb 4:12). "For as the rain and snow come down from heaven, and return not thither but water the earth, making it bring forth and sprout, giving seed to the sower and bread to the eater, so shall my word be that goes forth from my mouth; it shall not return to me empty, but shall accomplish that which I purpose, and prosper in the thing for which I sent it" (Is 55:10f).

It would therefore obviously not correspond with God's testimony with regard to the word he has uttered if we attempted simply to confront this word with God's work, and thus declare that the word is not work. Holy scripture ascribes power to the word just as it does to God's acts. We could even substitute for the psalm verse: "By the word of the Lord were the heavens made" (Ps 33 [32]:6) the statement: by God's work were the heavens made. Both statements would be correct, precisely because God's word is also his work in some way or other—in just what way we will later ascertain more clearly. And when in the first creation narrative (Gn 1:3–31) the divine word "Let there be" is immediately followed in every case by the statement "And there was," this divine word appears to be in fact more than a mere explanatory addition to God's activity. It looks much more as if the utterance of God's word were the actual action which effects the creation. So that if we distinguish God's word from his work at all, we must not conceive of the distinction in such a way that we fail to see that God's word has also the character of work.

But conversely, God's activity seems to have also the character of the word. What is peculiar to the word, namely that it brings knowledge to him to whom it is uttered, is in large measure peculiar also to that work God performs for men and on them. A quite considerable discussion has arisen in the Catholic world concerning the revealing character of the divine activity. God's extraordinary and miraculous activity joined with his revealing utterance has always had great importance for fundamental theology. This branch of theology defines God's revelation as "God's word of testimony," and therefore argues that God's word is the realization of his revelation in the true sense of the term. But fundamental theology has no intention of thus excluding God's activity. Its immedate intention however is to lend the legitimacy of divine authority to the human speech in which God's word is communicated to men—whether this be the speech of the Old Testament prophets or the New Testament apostles, or whether it be even the word of the God-man himself. But this interpretation fails in that the extraordinary and wonderful work which God's messenger performs is assigned a purely external and subservient role in relation to the promulgation of revelation itself. Revelation then seems to occur merely in the spoken word. By contrast the work performed in the power of God stands alongside revelation as a mere credential. The event of God's mighty act has inwardly and substantially nothing, or hardly anything, to do with revelation. It is intended only to serve as an external demonstration to those who are skeptical—with regard to the utterance of God's messenger—that an authority is being asserted here which the human messenger could not claim in his own person. The wonderful work would thus have merely the task of showing *that* God wishes to encounter man here. But what God wishes to say to man seems, according to this view, to be reserved for the word alone, a word spoken in his name by God's messenger.

This interpretation of the work, namely that its miraculous character demonstrates the divine origin of him who performs it, is quite natural for the apologist; moreover it has a considerable importance. But it is not legitimate to claim that this is the only significance of the work. This interpretation may be sufficient for apologetic purposes: in order to prove the divine origin of the word spoken by the messenger of revelation. The First Vatican Council also takes such a view in its consideration of the wonderful and, in purely human terms, inexplicable nature of the church's existence and character as confirming that the church is the messenger of divine revelation. "Only the Catholic church possesses all the many and wonderful signs which God has given, so that the credibility of Christian doctrine may shine forth brightly. Indeed, the church is in itself . . . a great and permanent motive of credibility and an irrefragable witness of its own divine sending."[17] In this statement the miraculous element in the church is not seen as part of God's self-revelation; thus the church is not considered as God's word. Rather the statement says what it is that gives the church a legitimate right, in its function as messenger communicating the word of God through its ministry of preaching, to demand men's faith. This right is granted to the church through the fact that its existence and character transcend created power and point therefore to God, who stands behind the church.

This marvelous and symbolic element is indeed a property of the church. But it is exterior to its ministerial function of communicating divine revelation. The divine work active in the church stands alongside the divine word communicated by the church. According to this view the communication of revelation actually occurs through the preaching of the word alone, whereas the marvelous appearance of God's work is here considered not as itself a part of revelation, but rather as proof of the fact that the church's word transmits the word of God with substantial accuracy.

This view, as we have already said, is possible and correct so long as it does not pretend to be the exhaustive interpretation of God's work in relation to his word. A proper understanding of divine revelation would resist any such pretense. It is being emphasized today, and quite rightly, that God's work does not merely stand alongside revelation as a criterion, but rather that it is itself an essential part of that concrete total reality in which God reveals himself to man. "According to the testimony of scripture God's acts in the drama of redemption are not merely criteria 'tacked on' to revelation—the almost exclusive view customary in fundamental theology; more than that, and in their essence, these divine acts are a form of revelation itself."[18]

That God's activity is an intrinsic part of his revelation is proclaimed by the word of God itself. For the communication of knowledge is ascribed to God's activity, which can thus be said to possess, in a certain sense, the character of a word. It is true that the divine work is still distinct from God's word, as we shall presently see, and that the two are not therefore simply identical. But at any rate holy scripture speaks in such a way that God's work appears to bear and communicate knowledge. This is true even of God's "natural" activity in his creation. We know of course that Paul appeals to this truth in his criticisms of the Gentiles. Because they have not received that form of God's self-revelation available even to men to whom God's revelation in the word has not yet come, still they have incurred the divine wrath and are in need of redemption. "The wrath of God is revealed from heaven against all ungodliness and wickedness of men who by their wickedness suppress the truth. For what can be known about God is plain to them, because God has shown it to them. Ever since the creation of the world his invisible nature, namely his eternal power and deity, has been clearly perceived in the things that have been made. So that they are without excuse" (Rom 1:18–20). "For all men who were ignorant of God were foolish by nature; and they were unable from the good things that are seen to know him who exists, nor did they recognize the craftsman while paying heed to his works; . . . If through delight in the beauty of these [created] things men assumed them to be gods, let them know how much better than these is their Lord, for the author of beauty created them" (Wis 13:1ff).

In the controversies of the previous century, in the face of which the First Vatican Council had to defend the truth of faith, a number of quite different attitudes led to the denial that created things could lead to the knowledge of God. In the proclamation of its teaching the church has been concerned to defend the task laid upon man's knowledge, and with it the potentiality of that knowledge, against these forms of skepticism. But in so doing the church has also safeguarded the profound dignity of the created world as a means of expression for God's self-disclosure. "God, the author and end of all things, can be known with certainty from created things by the natural light of human reason."[19] So runs the definition of the Vatican I (which also refers to Rom 1:20), thus rescuing the honor of human reason and interpreting the meaning of the created world. And the fact that God communicates himself in his work of creation is something of more than merely academic and abstract significance. On the contrary God intends to confront and to challenge man in this form of self-disclosure as well. In the proclamation of its teaching the church also delineates clearly the "prophetic" sense of the natural knowledge of God, a knowledge derived from the created world, by emphasizing along with the natural cognoscibility of God the natural moral law. Man can and should discern in the order of the created world in which he lives the decrees of the creator. "When the Gentiles who have not the [positive] law do by nature what the law requires, they are a law to themselves, even though they do not have the law" (Rom 2:14).[20]

But the divine activity which belongs to the supernatural order of salvation and grace also possesses, according to revelation, the function of conveying knowledge, and hence of God's word. What God effects by grace in the innermost depths of man cannot of course be directly experienced and is therefore not heard, as is a word. But precisely for this reason God has joined to his indiscernible *supernatural* activity, by which he communicates himself to man in grace, his visible *extraordinary* activity in history, in which he makes himself known in discernible manner. He arouses astonishment in men so that they may come to realize that beyond all the occurrences they can account for there is something going on which is a special intervention of God, something testifying to a divine communication that transcends any and every kind of closeness to God which is normal for men. Of frequent occurrence in the Old Testament are the interpretive words: "Thus shall you know that I am the Lord." This knowledge is to be won through experience of God's activity. For God's work is revelation, or at least an essential part of revelation. Hence John says of the first miracle Jesus performed: "This, the first of his signs, Jesus did at Cana in Galilee, and manifested his glory; and his disciples believed in him" (Jn 2:11).

Thus it is understandable that theology today is concerned in bringing word and work, as they occur in divine revelation, into close conjunction with one another. God's activity seems almost to be another kind of speech. God's work appears to be his word in another form. God's word is in the service of revelation; it is revelation's organ and means of expression. But we have seen that God reveals himself in his work as well. Hence God's work and his revelation also belong together. But since two things which are both linked with a third must also have a connection with each other, God's word and his work seem to be—at the very least—closely related facets of his revelation.

It is true that in the distinction often made between God's revelation through word and his revelation through work, the two seem once again to become separated. But in reality it is precisely this distinction which can confirm the intimate connection between God's word and his work. For the distinction between revelation through word and through work is determined merely by the form of expression in which the revelation is communicated to man's knowledge. Since word and work are two means of expressing one revelation they are thus joined in a higher unity.

It is evident then that despite the very close kinship between word and work it is still important to distinguish in just what way the word of God on the one hand and his work on the other impart his communication to men. It is now our task to ascertain the distinction between them, and to discern what it is that actually brings word and work together in a twofold unity in the act of revelation.

The Dissimilarity of Word and Work

Both God's word and his work are means by which God addresses himself to men. However the emphasis is different in each case. When God addresses himself to man in work he does so primarily to accomplish something in man or for him. The work always has above all an effectual significance. But because the work is performed meaningfully, proceeding from a plan and directed toward a goal, it is possible to discern the work's significance from its basic pattern. Thus the work also becomes the demonstration of its author's will. In the case of the word the emphasis is reversed. Its first significance is to communicate what is contained in one person's mind to another person. This occurs by way of knowledge, and through the attitude the will assumes when challenged by this knowledge. However man's personal and mental life is embedded in his total existence, which in turn has its roots in the world, wherein man lives and to which he gives living form. Therefore an effect which has the character of work is always linked indirectly with the word's communicating power.

But still, once again, we see that word and work have not only a certain common efficacy, but a certain common power of expression as well. Yet when we look at them more closely we discover that word and work express things in very different ways. If one of the partners in a dialog expresses himself in a work, the meeting of minds is achieved but haltingly, and may quite possibly remain partial. The work remains, at first, alone. When it has been performed it is taken out of its author's hand, so to speak, and may easily cease to be capable of joining its author and recipient with one another. The reason for this is intrinsic. For a work is really performed for the benefit it confers. Thus its end is determined quite objectively. The criterion then for judging the goodness of a work performed is whether in the framework of means and end it properly fulfills its function as a means of accomplishing something. Once the author has performed his work his own person is really no longer decisive in judging the work.

Now if someone, in order to communicate himself to another, makes use of a work which he performs, he must take into account the danger that he himself will be lost sight of, once the moment in which he has presented his work to the other is ended. As long as the donor's hands remain in contact with whatever he gives, or so long as even an accompanying word directs attention to the donor, the connection between his intention to give something and the gift he offers will not be overlooked. But once the act of presentation is over and the accompanying word is stilled, only the thing itself endures: the work in its objective reality. It is possible, as before, to recognize from the thing the connection with him who has performed it and given it. However such recognition does not occur directly, but little by little. We see the work with its characteristic properties. On the basis of this initial consideration and knowledge we recall not merely that the work was given to us and that it was offered by the donor as a present, but we remember also the character of the donor. It is in this way that man can and should see from the work of creation, as well as from the extraordinary work of God's miracles, that God exists and that he communicates himself. A work does not speak of him who, in the work, discloses himself with the same immediacy as does a word. A work requires a gradual process of inference which leads back from the work to its author. The work is a means: it and its principles must first be fully known. Then is it possible, from this knowledge, to arrive by inference to him who has performed the work (the "*medium ex quo*"). This connection between the work and its author proves often enough to be so loose that the superficial all too quickly lose sight of it. Or they may not even grasp the connection sufficiently in the first place, so that they fail to be led to the inevitable recognition of the divine master-workman and revealer.

There are, to be sure, also works which do proclaim their author more or less directly. Much as is the case with regard to the word, these works are not really performed in order to produce a physical effect. Rather they are intended to express an intention and to represent a reality. They come very close in function to the word, and are themselves a kind of word. These works are those acts or objects performed or produced in order to represent a sign or symbol, or to express something inward and hidden. Such a symbolic sign is a work effected by its author through his productive activity: he designs, groups, shapes his material. But it is not a work in the sense of the previous discussion. These signs and symbols do not really signify a practical value. They are addressed to man's understanding and challenge him to make a decision. They are work in the sense in which a word is also a work. For a word must of course always be formulated, and hence wrought, in order to be heard, read and understood. But this concerns merely the work's physical existence, not its significance and its task. Thus this kind of work does not belong to those means of expression which have the character of a work, and from which it is possible to infer the existence and character of their author. They belong far more to the category of the word. The word's function as a means of expression will be discussed presently.

The sacraments belong to this category of means of

expression with the character of work—a category which must actually be classified under the heading "word." Certainly the sacraments are intended to effect in man something supernatural which we call grace. But it is not at all easy to say just how the sacraments achieve this efficacy. At any rate we must not overlook the fact that the sacraments have primarily the function of signs and symbols addressed to man's understanding and to his will. To be sure, these signs are so charged with reality that they both contain and communicate that which they signify. But this realism must not be made so concrete that we overlook the symbolism present in the sacraments; it is because of this symbolism that the sacraments are a personal challenge to man—achieving their effect by their symbolic representation of this same effect.[21] The church, the basic sacrament, belongs also to these works in which God communicates himself through signs to man. The word of God is not merely administered in the church: in a genuine sense the church itself *is* God's word. And in the category of works in which God expresses himself belongs above all Christ, the God-man. He is God's word because we do not have to reason from him, in his appearance as man among men, to God. Rather in contemplating him we see God himself. When the apostles proclaim Christ they proclaim the word of life which is God. But they assure us that they proclaim that "which we have seen with our eyes, which we have looked upon and touched with our hands" (1 Jn 1:1).

So we have now distinguished the word as a means of expression used by God to disclose himself from the divine work. He who uses a single word to disclose himself to another, or many words joined together in a sentence or in a whole series of sentences, does not offer a work from which the other is intended to infer the author of this self-disclosure. Rather the meaning intended by the speaker is put forward in the word without any process of logical deduction. The word and the full sentence are like a body with many members: the meaning is like the soul, fashioning the whole into a living unity. And the speaker always has a share in the peculiar strength of the divine communication, that utterance of the word in which the Father expresses himself within the Godhead. The speaker also shares always in God's creative activity. For God does not adopt and use a ready-made expression. On the contrary he first brings the expression into being in creative utterance.

It is true that man, in uttering an individual word, is hardly creative at all. The individual word has a soul, a meaning that is there, once and for all, in the work. Man can adopt this meaning if he will: he cannot create it. But actual speech is of course more than the employment of an individual word. Speech consists in the speaker's arrangement of the individual words in such a way that their content and meaning transcend that of the words taken separately. By the way he puts his words together the speaker expresses himself in a very personal manner as the man that he is. Above and beyond the general manner in which the words of any given language convey the meaning and opinion of the speaker, the individual expresses himself in a very special way through his style. *Le style c'est l'homme.* The word spoken by any given man expresses more fully what is in him than does a work, for a work always remains to some extent at least anonymous. And when a man has fashioned his words into a whole they characterize him to a degree which one could never expect from an examination of the individual words themselves. So that when we speak of the word as the means by which a person who has something to communicate expresses himself, we must think not of the individual words but rather of the words as fashioned together into a living whole and animated with a soul by the creative skill of the speaker.

This observation, that the style of expression has a quite personal depth of meaning which lies beneath the immediate meaning of the individual words, has a special parallel in the case of God's word. Here the hidden meaning lies much deeper. It can be plumbed only under the guidance of the Holy Spirit, whom God sends to his church for this purpose. It is the deeper meaning that God hides beneath the words used by those human authors to whom his inspiration and revelation are addressed; and whose writings, because they are, after all, human, must be understood first of all in their human sense. Of course the deeper meaning intended by God cannot be foreign to the human sense, much less contradictory to it. It would be nonsense to speak of God's word in the humanly framed utterances of the prophets, the apostles or holy scripture if the immediate and humanly ascertainable sense of these writings did not at least point toward, and give a glimpse of, those depths in which God has hidden this deeper meaning. But it is the Holy Spirit, permeating and guiding the church so that it may be capable of plumbing the divine depths of the word of God, who is responsible for the actual recognition of this deeper and hidden meaning of scripture. Just as in the purely natural sphere a certain sympathy is necessary for the appreciation and evaluation of expressive skill and style, so also in the church do we need that supernatural sympathy imparted by the Holy Spirit if we are to grasp fully in the word of God as it is proclaimed that deeper meaning which is given to it by the Spirit.

The word therefore is not, as is a work, the beginning of a process of reasoning which leads us to the author of the work. The significance of the word dwells in the word far more as the soul dwells in its body. The word conveys its intended meaning much more immediately than a work could ever do—unless of course the author's signature were engraved upon the work. But in that case it would no longer be a mere work but at the same time a word.

Now because we have spoken here of how work and word are at the same time similar and different with respect to God's revelation in work and word, we must add something more. The fact that work and word cannot simply be equated with one another must not lead us to the conclusion that the two do not have much in common with one another within the total occurrence of divine revelation. Nor should the impression arise that God's work and word are equal but distinct kinds of divine revelation. On the contrary: we have here set forth the difference between God's work and word precisely in order to demonstrate what they have in common in their service of divine revelation. That is to say, the two are not actually two modes of divine revelation, as might be suggested by the distinction between revelation in work and revelation in word. In reality God's work and his word (both in the natural order and in the supernatural order of grace) constitute two essential elements of a single act of revelation.

The biblical revelation leaves no doubt that the word in which God communicates himself is in fact always linked effectually with his creative activity, or at least that this is ideally the case. This is of course that special characteristic of that love in which God communicates himself to man. He does not turn in love toward man as he exists only after and because man has shown himself to be worthy of love. Quite the opposite. God creates for himself a partner worthy of love by communicating himself in love. This is also true of that word in which God turns toward his human partner. God's salutation is creative. Through the fact that God addresses his word to man, man achieves his reality and existence. Thus Vatican I has brought out the fact that creation's meaning and end is the manifestation of the divine perfection.[22] Thus this divine self-revelation is given priority over his work in creation by being designated its end and goal. Naturally there is no point to a manifestation if it cannot be recognized, accepted and answered. It assumes therefore the rational partner, man, to whom God's goodness is communicated in creation. This does not mean however that the human partner first came into being in a purely objective manner, and that God's goodness was only then communicated to him. No: in the communication of the divine goodness God's human partner achieves his being vis-à-vis God. This applies also to God's manifestation of himself in word. Creative activity is also linked with the utterance of the divine word.

The biblical revelation, conversely, teaches us that God's activity never occurs apart from his word. "By the word of the Lord were the heavens made" (Ps 33[32]:6). When God created the world he spoke: "Let there be." His work in the whole process of redemption is always linked with his work spoken through the mouth of the prophets. The highest realization of his work in Jesus Christ is at the same time the consummation of his word to men.

The point however is not merely that God's work and his word are always linked with one another. What is important is that they penetrate one another inwardly as two essential elements of God's one revelation. God's work is the material element in the revelation. It is that in which God communicates himself to men by "going out of himself." But God's work needs a kind of soul, a determinative element, to make absolutely clear its character as revelation and as personal communication and to direct it to man's faculties of understanding and decision. This element is given God's work by his word. The word is the formal element in revelation. It is for God's revelation what the soul is for the living man, whereas God's work is for his revelation what the body is for man. Just as the soul is not the man without the body, nor the body without the soul, but only the embodied soul or the animated body, so also is this the case of God's revelation: it occurs in inner, living unity between God's work and his word. God's revelation is his work, to which the word imparts clarity and personal character. Or God's revelation is the word which has its creative fullness in work.

It may be asked which of these two elements is actually more important for the redemptive significance of divine revelation: the work, in which God's communication proves to be efficacious, or the word, which imparts to revelation the personal fullness of meaning that touches man inwardly. Although such a question would not be entirely easy to answer, it is actually pointless. In the order of salvation both are important. And it must necessarily prove to be fatal when an importance is ascribed to one element at the expense of the other. We must not make of the work something so effectual that there is no more room for man's free decision. But we must also refrain from trying to interpret everything in terms of the word, which would then be overlooking God's effectual activity over and above the utterance. The word and the work serve one another within the framework of God's revelation. The two taken together constitute the one divine revelation in its fullness.

The connection of work and word is shown very clearly in the history of God's redemptive activity. The climax of this activity, the appearance and work of the incarnate word of God, joins work and word in a single unity. The work of the incarnation is interpreted by the word of the angels. When Christ allows the work of baptism to be performed on him by John the word, in the form of the voice from heaven, bears witness that this man who has just received baptism is no sinner, but the well beloved Son of the Father. The event which is made manifest to the disciples in the ambiguity of the empty tomb is interpreted by the angel's word as the master's resurrection. On Pentecost Peter demonstrates through the words of his sermon that what has made the disciples drunk is their being filled with the Holy Spirit. The word certifies God's work and raises it from its ambiguity into the clarity of God's demand.

The special significance of God's word, which is not merely attached to the work but which penetrates it innerly as a saving act, consists in the fact that this word transforms the anonymity and impersonal character which somehow always cling to a work into a gift of God to men. This becomes clear from the first narrative of creation. Because the whole six-day creation comes to a climax and reaches its greatest significance in the creation of man, the creation of each work is introduced with the word. This word, it is true, does at first seem to reflect the consultation within the Godhead, or to be also a word of command, calling the work into being out of nothing. But at the end of the narrative the word is addressed to man, for whom the work of the world is performed. Through the animating word the work itself becomes a word of salutation to man.

When men give each other presents on some festive occasion the gift has, as a thing, at first an impersonal character, as does the work from which it originates. The gift becomes a true salutation addressed to the recipient only through the word with which the giver presents his gift. In the same way God gives to the work of his creation—in which he remains so hidden that even alert and sensitive men can keep alive the recollection of the creator's active hand only by conscious effort—the personal character of a salutation that accompanies a gift by affixing to his work his word. In holy scripture, in contrast to the Greek idea of the Logos, the word of God has far more the character of a salutation than of the communication of new knowledge. We should certainly not play off one against the other, as Rudolf Bultmann seems to do, as though "God's words in the Old Testament . . ." were "not a theological doctrine, an ideology to be pondered, understood and adopted."[23] Such a blank assertion that the bible denies to the word any theoretical or contemplative sense is also false. After all, the salutation always needs a minimum of objective content and doctrinal character. However it is probably beyond all doubt that the word of God, as understood in both the Old and New Testaments, "proclaims the will of God; his word is salutation, a summons to decision." This anthropological character of God's word can very well be pointed up and described as follows: "God's word characterizes God as he is present for, and perceptible by, man. God's word is God, insofar as he calls man into being, establishes his limits and in a mysterious manner embraces him."[24]

God's word then is not merely affixed to his work. It is the work's soul, that alone which makes of the work what it is truly intended to be in God's plan of redemption: a work performed for man and on man. Therefore man can do God's work no greater injustice than to allow it to become an impediment to his encounter with God. For in reality it is his duty to hear God's word in his work, and to answer it by imitating the divine work in his own creative activity in the world.

3 God's Word and Man's Reply

Apart from the paired notions of God's word and revelation, and his word and work, there is still a third pair which must be discussed in order to clarify and determine what

God's word really is. This pair comprises the uncomplementary parts: God's word and man's reply. A special importance is attached to precisely this question in the controversial discussion between the Catholic and Protestant confessions. For an interpretation of the relationship of man to God the double unity of word and reply is extraordinarily important. Contesting the one-sided Reformation emphasis on the proclamation of God's word as the only means of mediating salvation is the emphasis (not, incidentally, so one-sided) on the sacrament. And this is important because God's word leaves the way open, and demands a genuine reply from men in the sacrifice of the God-man. Protestantism, in allowing room only for the word and its acceptance in faith, considered as the bearer of the salvation freely given by God, has no sufficient understanding of the significance of man's answer for his salvation; it has therefore an insufficient understanding of a personal encounter between God and man.

The Reformation is in danger of interpreting the relationship of God and man only in the descending and downward line, and of neglecting the upward and ascending direction of man's reply. Thus the cross stands in the middle of the reformed doctrine of the redemption; but it is not sufficiently understood as the act in which the God-*man* replies to the Father. It is considered rather as the gift of the Father, who gave his Son up to death for man. In the doctrine of justification the saving effect of grace is not understood as that which makes man capable of meritorious work in answer to God's communication of grace. The Christian notion of agape is supposed to have been repurified by Luther from its mixture with elements of the Greek eros. According to this view eros is a human deed which ascends to the divinity, whereas the New Testament concept of agape, which Luther allegedly restored, is of something spontaneously given by God to man here below; man must respond by handing on this gift to his fellowmen.[25] The train of theological thought emphasizing the action of God "alone" must then interpret the sacrament too as merely another kind of sermon which comes down as a proclamation from above, but not as an action with a response in the other direction, from below upward.

It is true that there is a complex understanding of God's word which, in addition to the salutation addressed to man by God, includes men's reply to God as well. But this must not lead us to overlook the fact that in this complex understanding of God's word there is still, and always, the dialog pattern of word and reply. There is in other words an understanding of God's word in the narrower and probably more genuine sense which distinguishes this word from the word of answer which complements it. Both must be kept in view.

The Human Reply as God's Word

Everyone knows what an echo is. You call out your words and wait for the reverberation. The shouted word and the echo which comes back proceed in different directions. But we do not call the echo a true reply to the word shouted by the speaker. On the contrary the speaker recognizes his own word in the echo just as in his call. For a reply assumes various things not contained in an echo. Indeed reply has a content inwardly linked with what has been said in the original word, but it is still different from this word: it is its continuation and complement. And the reason is quite simply that the word which is answered was not uttered against a wall that merely, physically throws back the sound waves. The word was spoken to an understanding man, who receives the word in himself and who in a mental decision gives the reply. Here word and reply are distinguished. In the case of the echo such a distinction is meaningless. At most we can distinguish between the sounding and resounding of the one word.

We wanted to discuss here an understanding of the concept of God's word which also includes the reply that comes back; an understanding therefore which characterizes the entire process of God's speaking and man's answer. Such an understanding cannot, as we have seen, be based on the example of the echo. The echo is not a reply. It does not contain any word formed by the partner of a conversation on the basis of the word which he had heard, and uttered by him in response. When on the other hand God sends forth his word to man, he addresses man's hearing and his faculty of free decision; and he wants a reply. And God's word leaves man free to give his reply or to refuse it, and to reply in one way or in another. Therefore even if it is really possible to find a reason for including in the notion of God's word also man's reply, this reason must be different from what obtains in the case of the echo.

But there is nevertheless a similarity. God's communication has such a powerful effect upon the reply that man gives to the divine word that ground can be found here for terming the reply returned by man God's word too. If everything by which someone bears witness to another of what lies hidden in the secret recesses of his being is described as word, then it is in fact possible to call the reply that man makes to God's word also the word of the revealing God.

This is justified by the very fact that man's reply testifies that God has spoken to him and that God's word has effected something in him. A life of devotion to God, in God's service, and of witness for God is a life of faith. But faith is that kind of hearing in which man takes God's revealing speech into his own personal inner realm so that he may make his decisions on the basis of this revelation. A life of faith is therefore like an echo, or better . . . like a reply to God's word. Thus the divine word also resounds in such a life at all times, because and insofar as it is an answering life.

But the reason it is possible to consider even man's reply as being still God's word lies deeper yet. The word which goes forth from God must of course be seen in close association with the divine work. God's word is, to be sure, not identical with his work. But in the redemptive order the two are very intimately connected. The word stands alongside God's work not merely to interpret it and certify its character as a personal gift. In holy scripture God's word appears as a messenger sent by God to perform God's work. "He sends forth his commandment upon earth, and his word runs very swiftly. He gives snow like wool, and scatters the hoar-frost like ashes. He casts forth his ice like morsels, who is able to abide his frost? He sends out his word and melts them: he blows with his wind, and the waters flow" (Ps 147:15–18). And when the word means the revelation in Christ, then with this word is linked always God's effectual communication of himself, which, as grace, imparts to the acceptance of the word a strength transcending all humanly calculable reasons of credibility. Thus Vatican I says: "To this testimony [given by the church] is added effectual help from the power on high. For the most gracious God both awakes the erring with his grace and helps them 'to come to the knowledge of the truth' (1 Tim 2:4); and he strengthens with his grace those whom 'he has called out of darkness into his own marvelous light' (1 Pt 2:9), so that they may continue in this light, never deserting them unless they desert him."[26] This connection between the promulgated word of revelation and the work of God's grace, which effects faith, can be expressed then by seeing the word and the work of grace as identical and by calling both the divine word.

It is therefore understandable that in the notion of God's word the distinction between the word and man's reply is occasionally and to a certain extent veiled. For when seen in the light indicated immediately above man's reply is also God's work and, because it is a communication, it is in an analogous sense his word. There is no natural or supernatural kind of being or action in the creature which does not partake of God's being and action. God raises his creature into being by giving him a share of his own being. The creature's being and action thus proclaim the free self-giving of the eternal creator. In virtue of God's creative communication of himself man's possession is a genuine one. But he also has the duty of knowing and recognizing this God who makes himself known in his being, and of possessing his own human being as a revelation of God, as God's word. In fulfilling this duty man is obliged to return to the eternal creator the reply which corresponds to God's creative act. This reply is created man's own deed, for he has genuine possession of the being and capability God gives him. And yet his possession of these things is not so complete as to enable him to reply with that same fullness of initiative which belongs to God when he communicates himself in his word. In the mutual relationship of God and man the reply which ascends from man's depths to God is also the work of that God who upholds man in his being and who penetrates his actions. Insofar the reply of man also belongs at all times to that word in which God manifests himself with power.

The deeds performed in grace by a man who has been sanctified by Christ are his own. Otherwise they could not be reckoned as meritorious and rewarded with eternal salvation. What he does therefore is his reply to God's communication. But this does not mean that the man's own acts are called forth by God's word, but performed without God. Actually man's answering deed, no matter how much his own, is always at the same time God's deed. It is the Holy Spirit who calls within the man in a state of grace: "Abba, Father" (Rom 8:15; Gal 4:6). And when we read in the Apocalypse: "The Spirit and the bride say, Come" (Ap 22:17), this is not actually the twofold cry of two speakers, but rather God's Spirit, who awakes the cry of longing in the church, without this cry's ceasing to be the church's own. In its doctrine of merit the Council of Trent parried the claim that good works are merely from God without being man's own. But it is naturally assumed that they are in fact always God's work as well. "If anyone says that the good works of a justified man are gifts of God to such an extent that they are not also the good merits of the justified person himself; or that the justified person, through the good works that he does through divine grace and the merits of Jesus Christ, whose living member he is, does not actually merit increase of grace, eternal life and, if he dies in grace, entrance into this eternal life: let him be anathema."[27] Those works whose orientation is from man to God, in whose service they are of course performed, are also a demonstration of God's efficacy in grace and belong as such to God's work.

In this way even Christ's death on the cross, although it was something which ascended on high from below as an act of the God-man's obedience and as the creature's sacrifice offered to the eternal Lord, was nevertheless a manifestation of God himself, working in the God-man. "Jesus' prophecy of his passion, death, and resurrection is characterized by the words, *tón lógon laleîn* (to speak the word)—the same expression used in Mk 2:2. The statement is understandable only if we assume that Jesus (and resurrection) are considered the climax and fulfillment of revelation. . . . As death is the climax of revelation, so the preaching of his death by Jesus is the climax for God's *logos* of which he is the bearer. Indeed the preaching of death is quite simply *ho lógos.* Here the connection of the concept 'word of God' with the Old Testament appears as clearly as its distinction from the Old Testament concept. The 'word' in our passage is, as in the Old Testament, the divine word of revelation. However here God's revelation has an entirely different content from that which it possesses in the Old Testament. God reveals himself by giving his Son, the Messiah, over to suffering and death and by having him rise subsequently from the dead. It is precisely through this act of revelation that God fulfills his rule. And the word which reveals God's rule and which compels men to a decision is therefore the word of Jesus' death and resurrection."[28]

And in the Old Testament "it is not merely the proclamation of the redemptive acts and sayings of God . . . and not merely God's teachings and warnings to his people as contained in the words of the prophets which are God's word, but the sacred hymns come also from the Holy Spirit. . . . The temple liturgy had, thus, a lofty dignity. It was performed for the God who was invisibly present above the ark of the covenant, who made himself known in his word, and who was worshiped in the word which he had given to his people and in the sacrifices and rites which he had commanded."[29]

This is then a more comprehensive meaning and use of God's word, one which disregards the distinction between word and reply, precisely because the human reply is also a divine work containing God's proclamation of himself. But it is impossible for this very reason to deny this distinction. No matter how well justified this way of looking at the matter is, we must not overlook the fact that this comprehensive notion of God's word contains the two elements of word and reply. For what man says and does in reply to God is, quite simply, not so completely God's work and word that it is no longer in any real sense man's own deed and reply.

Word and Reply

If we were to content ourselves with the more comprehensive meaning of the concept of God's word which we have just discussed—and which, just because it is so broad, is actually not the exact meaning of the concept—there would not be much point in posing the question of man's reply, cooperation and discipleship when confronted with the call of God's word. However to forego in this way the consideration of the human answer would contradict the statements of divine revelation. It is not only to refute the charge of having done ill to his people that God demands: "Answer me" (Mi 6:3). Despite the emphasis on God's sovereign power the relationship of Yahweh to his people is still portrayed as one of genuine partnership, and as a dialog. The people of God are linked with him in a relationship which is called a testament, "*diatheke,*" that is, something established by God. But this relationship remains nevertheless that of a two-sided covenant. And the bible is especially fond of portraying this relationship under the metaphor of the deepest and most intimate realization of the covenant relationship: marriage. God speaks to his people and demands an answer. And his people cries out to him in supplication and in complaint confident of his answer. And so the theological consideration of the divine word must take this notion from its more comprehensive meaning back to a narrower one, in which the word is distinguished from the answer, God's condescending activity from the upward striving activity of men, God's call from men's hearing and following. Within the meaning of God's word which embraces both God's condescension and man's ascent we must always remember that we are speaking of something with the character of a dialog. In this dialog God, who acts on His own initiative, and man, acting in response, stand opposite one another, so that man's good work is a gift of divine grace, and yet remains also man's own merit.

That the proper sense of the term "word" demands its distinction from the answer is shown by a simple consideration of the two phenomena themselves. The essence of a word is that a person expresses something lying hidden inside him. And he does this not for the sake of the expression itself, but for the sake of communication with another person. Certainly the speaker is himself in a certain sense the goal which is to be fulfilled in his verbal communication. In the case of God's speech outside himself it is obvious that nothing outside himself can be the goal and aim of his communication. He can be impelled to action only by himself. But human conversation also shares imperfectly in this quality of purpose whose perfect realization is found in God alone. The word addressed to the other partner of the conversation has at the same time its goal in the speaker himself. He himself wants to be enriched by the word he speaks to the other. But it is not directly through the return of his own spoken word to him that the speaker is enriched. That may be the case in a purely internal, mental conversation, where the thinking man is in a sense his own interlocutor, and utters his thoughts to himself. But this is not a conversation in the true sense of the term. In a conversational exchange with an opposing interlocutor the word addressed to the other does indeed also address the speaker himself. But it is not the spoken word itself which is supposed to come back directly to the speaker. Rather does it produce its practical and reciprocal effect upon the speaker by causing him whom he addresses to recognize something and to react to it. And this reaction comes back to the speaker in the answer.

Precisely because in a conversation the goal of the speaker's words is also himself, his words must still reach the other first and be received by him. The word does not seek to be received back again as an echo, but as an answer. The interlocutor stands opposite the speaker. And only in that degree to which the speaker takes the interlocutor seriously as someone whom he encounters and as a person dominating the area of his own life, and aims at him in the conversation —only to this degree can the speaker expect an answer from his interlocutor and through this answer his own enrichment.

If this is the case however then word and answer cannot be the same. On the contrary it is then necessary to distinguish the double form and the two phases of the conversational process. The word does not at all achieve its intended effect when it does not come back from him to whom it is addressed to its speaker in another form, that is, in the form of the answer. If the word is to achieve its purpose there must be two partners who are joined with one another in a word having the double form of speech and rejoinder. The difference between the two partners and the fact that they stand opposite one another is reflected in the dual unity of word and answer, in the two phases back and forth, which join the two one with the other. The free decision to enter into reciprocal communication is preserved by the fact that the one does not work upon the other in an objective and anonymous act and through purely effectual power, but that he knocks on the other's door with a word, so that the other may freely open and give his reply.

It is not surprising therefore that the sources of revelation between God and man also speak to us of God's word in order to present man in the answer and to call forth this answer. It is possible in an analogous sense, as we have already remarked at an earlier stage, also to consider the work of divine creation as a kind of word, for in this work God communicates himself in recognizable form to man. The creation was not called into being for its own sake, but as God's personal work for a personal partner. The creation is wrought for man. He is summoned through this work to discern God's plan and intention in creation and recognize them by responding to them. The utterance of creation calls man's attention so emphatically to a personal, intelligent author that he must really expect that this author will now address him in a special word as well. For when the consideration of the existing world with a view to discovering its author causes man to recognize that this author is intelligent and personal, then this means that this author can also, precisely because he is a person, communicate himself to man in a more direct manner than is possible through his works alone. It is as if one were to receive a lovingly packed gift sent by a dear friend for some festive occasion. Simply from the way that the gift was chosen, arranged and packed it is possible to infer the person and attitude of the sender. But just for this reason one is immediately on the lookout for an accompanying letter which will express in the form of the personal word what is to a certain extent already recognizable in the impersonal gift. So also the recognition of God from his creation leads to the expectation of a revelation in word, in which God also addresses directly the man to whom he has given his works.[30]

The biblical revelation makes it clear that the point of

the work of creation is above all that it must be answered because it is God's communication to man. This answer occurs first of all when God is praised for his creation. "Rejoice in Yahweh, O you righteous! Praise befits the upright . . . Sing him a new song . . . For the word of Yahweh is true and all his works are faithful. He loves righteousness and justice; the earth is full of his goodness. By the word of Yahweh were the heavens made; and all the host of them by the breath of his mouth" (Ps 33[32]:1–6). Such praise is the answer to what God has sent man in his creation as work and word. Just as God's creative word takes concrete form in his work, so the word of praise uttered by man in his answer must also take concrete form in the work of shaping man's life. Man must answer the divine act of creation through the service of his work performed among creatures. "Whether you eat or drink, or whatever you do, do all to the glory of God" (1 Cor 10:31). Man, by discerning in the creature the order imprinted on his creation by God and by fashioning his intercourse with the creature in accordance with this order, hears and answers the communication God has made, since God has created the world for man.

The fact that word and answer, although distinct, are at the same time oriented to one another is shown especially in the redemptive event which Jesus Christ both is and which he effects. Here of course God's word came to us in the fullest sense. Holy scripture testifies that that event in which God's Son is the word of the Father to men stands in a dialog opposite that other event in which the God-man is man's answer to God. John says this in the form of a program when he introduces the narrative of Christ's sacrificial death with the words: "Since he knew that he . . . had come from God and was going to God . . ." (Jn 13,3). This statement interprets the death of the cross as an event which is part of a total process having the character of a dialog: the cross is the entrance into a sacrifice offered in order that the coming of the word in the incarnation may be answered.

Of course we can say that the incarnation of the son prepares the sacrifice of the cross. Paul seems to have taken this view, especially in his major epistles. "The incarnation has for Paul [it is the major epistles which are meant here] a redemptive significance only as the indispensable prerequisite for the death on the cross."[31] "God sent forth his son, born of a woman, born under the law, *so that* he could redeem those who were under the law, so that we might receive adoption as sons" (Gal 4:4f). In other words the real reason why the Father sent forth the Son in the incarnation was that the Son might offer the redemptive atoning sacrifice. But it is necessary to see in what way the incarnation actually achieves its significance as the preparation for the death of the cross. The incarnation is the preparation for the cross not merely because it supplies him who is then redemptively active in his divine and human life and death. In that case the incarnation itself would have no essential redemptive significance at all, but would simply be the necessary prerequisite for redemption. In reality however the incarnation itself is at the same time also an essential part of a total process having the character of a dialog. The first part of this process is the prerequisite and condition of the second; and its second part is the continuation and fulfillment of the first. Both parts, taken in their totality, are the source of redemption. In his redemptive activity God unites with himself the human race which has been separated from him. He does so by means of an effectual redemptive dialog which is initiated by his word to men, and which finds its completion in the answering sacrifice. The sacrifice of the God-man on the cross is the answer to that word which appeared on earth in the incarnation as God's Son. The death on the cross is the sacrifice for the sins of the world. And in this sacrifice the Lord ascends as man's answer to God after having appeared to man in the incarnation as God's spokesman. Pius XII has spoken of this fact in connection with his interpretation of the part played by the priest as Christ's representative in the church's liturgy. "In virtue of the sacerdotal power the priest portrays the person of Jesus Christ to the people whom he represents. Before God however he stands as representative of this same people . . . The priest, prior to his appearance before God in the name of the people, is already the ambassador of the divine Savior; and because Jesus Christ is the head of that body of which the faithful are members, the priest represents God to the people entrusted to him."[32] In his sacrifice Christ carries out, as head of the human race, man's surrender to God; whereas in the incarnation and in the church's preaching, which is its continuation, he has presented to us the God who comes to man to be received in faith.

This pattern in the saving act which has been accomplished for mankind is reflected also in the individual's redemption. According to a concept much beloved by the fathers the Logos is born in the soul of man through the grace of justification; the individual conceives the divine word.[33] The meritorious work man is subsequently able to perform is then nothing other than his participation in the answer made by the God-man in the sacrifice of the cross. Both things belong in the same manner to the redeemed life. They are not identical however, but are distinguished as word and answer.

The fact that word and answer are different, as in a dialog, is confirmed by subjecting the proposition to a counter-test of its negative: the answer can fail, even though the word has been uttered. Here is the significance of the manifold controversies in which the church and its theologians have attempted to clarify the relationship of divine grace and human freedom. What was at stake was the character of human behavior before God as a genuine answer. Against the Pelagianism and Semi-Pelagianism of all ages, for which man's own decision alone is crucial, the church has had to defend the efficacy of God's grace. But on the other hand the church has had to oppose those who have considered it impossible to guard God's dominant role without denying the freedom of man's will and his partnership with God. Therefore the Council of Trent proclaimed in a single paragraph that "in adults the beginning of justification lies in the prevenient grace of God through Jesus Christ, that is, in his call, which summons them without any previous merit of their own at all." But the council continues in just as sharp a tone to say that "those who had turned aside from God through their sins are disposed through his stimulating and helping grace to turn toward their own justification by freely assenting to this grace and by cooperating with it." And that there might be no uncertainty as to what was meant by the word "free" the council continues: "When God thus touches the heart of man through the illumination of the Holy Spirit, man is, on the one hand, not totally inactive, since he accepts this inspiration which he could also reject; but on the other hand he is unable of his own free will without the grace of God to arise to righteousness before God."[34]

It is not easy to explain this relationship between grace and man's own decision. If it is interpreted in the sense of the word, or of a call, as the council puts it, which is issued to man in grace, and of the answer man gives, even though he could also refuse it, it is easy to take an all too objective view of grace. The attempts to interpret the relationship between grace and freedom have been complicated by the fact that such attempts have assumed a somewhat material conception of grace, whereas God's grace is capable of penetrating man's will so deeply that it brings all the will's characteristics, including its freedom, to their fulfillment. The more man's will is penetrated by the God of grace the more fully is he able to share in the fulfillment of the blessed, whose freedom excludes the possibility of sinning. We must guard ourselves therefore against a too material view of grace and the human will when we interpret man's decision as an answer to God's call. But on the other hand we must not conceive of the entrance of grace into the human will as something by which God identifies himself with, and abolishes, the independence of his human interlocutor. It is necessary to preserve the distinction between word and answer, God's work of grace and man's cooperation, God's call and man's acceptance of the call. Just because man "could also reject this inspiration" there is no room for doubt that we are dealing here with a process having the character of a dialog in the proper sense of the term, a dialog in which the answer is not refused. For this reason God joins to his work of grace in man the word of his revelation, so that what happens in justification may be recognized as essentially a dialog. Grace itself cannot of course be apprehended as a call or a salutation. Therefore the work of grace itself cannot actually be described as a call which seeks an answer. The good work in which man gives his assent to grace can be cooperation only if man knows of God's work of grace. But he can know of this only if God's work, in itself unknowable, is made recognizable and answerable through the word of revelation.

This truth of faith, that God's word and grace can remain without man's assent, confirms the fact that word and answer, God's descent to us men and man's ascent in devotion to God, are not the same. And so within the framework of a conception of God's word and work which also includes the answer we must not overlook the contrast between word and answer, work and cooperation.

3 God's Word in the Church

God's word does not rest, once it has been promulgated, like some great static object. It is directed at a target, and that target is man. This is true of God's actual and most complete revelation of himself in the God-man, Jesus Christ. But it also applies to all the other ways in which God's word is promulgated: for they are all images of the incarnation. The personal word of God is even in its existence with the Godhead certainly not something static and at rest, but points back simply to the Father who in his utterance establishes his word with the Godhead. This disposition of the original word within the Godhead also sets the pattern for the incarnate word of God, uttered outwardly and directed at a target. By being promulgated God's incarnate word creates salvation. But salvation is a reality for men. Thus God's word is a salutation directed at men.

It is certainly the case that this listening acceptance of the divine word by men must occur in individuals. The bodily ear, but also the mind's ear, is not a collective organ of the community as such. On the contrary it belongs to the individual. And of course salvation too is supposed to thrust through to the individual by his hearing of the divine word. Salvation and damnation are attained in the free decision of man for or against God. But free decision is always the affair of the individual man.

The observation made by cultural historians that Christianity gives increased importance to the human person—not only to those of certain classes but to all men—is a reflection of Christianity's reality penetrating man's natural existence. For in the realm of life for God and in God the central conviction of the Christian faith is that God's fatherly love embraces each individual man as his child. In the Lord's Prayer it is not a collective child which prays "Our Father;" rather a community of God's children confesses its multiple unity in the face of "our" Father. Thus each individual man who is addressed in Christ hears the word uttered to him by the Father.

The question now however is how God's word reaches its target in the individual man: whether it comes directly to the individual or through the fellowship of the church. Does the fellowship of those who hear and follow God's word arise as the result of the discipleship of many individuals who, like the spokes of a wheel, come ever closer to one another the nearer they come to the center, to the summoning word of God? Or is God's word of revelation received first and directly by the church, so that the individual must enter this community in order to share in the hearing of God's word? The question can also be posed as follows: is God's word promulgated charismatically to each individual, or is it something institutional, made objective, established permanently in the church in order that it may (to be sure) again and again achieve fresh life in the individual?

The question is the same as that which distinguishes the Catholic understanding of the church from most non-Catholic conceptions of what the church is. Is it really true that the "legally organized church as such can never be the church of Christ; that it can therefore never speak in the name of Christ's church, never assert its rules as the rule of Christ's church, or the rule of Christendom's life with God, because the church of Christ transcends every legal order?"[35]

And this because "the people of God in the New Testament is a spiritual people; children of God, not children of Abraham. It is the Spirit of God which makes men God's children. There lies the essence of Christianity. The Spirit of God rules the people of God. But the Spirit of God is in every Christian . . . Therefore in the New Testament Israel theocracy is expressed . . . exclusively as 'pneumatocracy,' not in the form of law and decree."[36] Is the church really "the sum of the individual believers"? This formulation is found in a list of various conceptions of the church[37] as a description of the "Protestant individualism" which Emil Brunner contrasts with the alleged "Catholic collectivism."[38]

God's word is in fact issued to individuals through the community to which the word is directed. Even Emil Brunner, who declines to recognize the church in Christ's references to the ecclesia in the gospels, emphasizes: "Between the word of Christ and faith there can be no dispute about which was first; for faith is the answer to Christ's word. This word is entrusted to the community . . . Therefore Jesus' community precedes each of the faithful as the *mater piorum*."[39]

Let us now pursue the ecclesiastical character of God's word, and therefore its quality as something to be proclaimed, in the various stages of the drama of redemption: in the realm of the Old Testament church before the Church, and above all in the Church which, because it is the community of those who hear and follow God's word, mediates salvation to the individual.

1 God's Word in the Period before the Church

In the doctrine of the sacred signs which, through being performed on man who receives them according to their symbolical meaning, accomplish his salvation, theology also discusses the question whether there were already sacraments in the Old Testament. This question follows upon the conviction that there was already a church before the Church. The Old Testament *kahal* is the preparatory redemptive community which finds its fulfillment and full realization in the church founded by Christ. The fathers frequently trace this Old Testament "church" back to Abel.[40] Abel is a type of Christ because he too was put to death, and because he is a primal figure in the redemptive community of the Old Testament. The Old Testament also had a sign instituted by God through which membership in the redeeming people was imparted and accomplished. The Council of Florence in its Decree for the Armenians brought out the difference between the sacraments of the Old and New Testaments, declaring that it consists in the fact that "the former did not effect grace, but merely foreshadowed the grace which would be given through the passion of Christ; our sacraments, however, both contain grace and impart it to those who receive the sacraments worthily."[41] At the same time however the council made it clear that even here it was speaking of sacraments, and thereby confirmed the affinity between the people of the covenant in the Old Testament and the church of the New Testament. And the fact that the Old Testament community mediated grace is confirmed by the common opinion of theologians that the circumcision effected "*ex opere operato*" incorporation into the redemption the people of the old covenant, whose life prepared the faithful to share in the promises made to the people of God.

It is already clear from what we have observed that God's communication to man in grace and word is not issued to individuals in individualistic multiplicity, but rather to the people as a whole, and then to the individual because of his membership in this people. The word in which God communicates himself to the individual has already been received prior to the individual who hears it, and it is institutionally preserved. This can be discerned even before the existence of Christ's church in the various ways in which the divine word was promulgated.

Creation and History

According to dogma formulated by the First Vatican Council, God can be discerned by natural reason in creation. The created world is therefore a proclamation of God, but not with the same immediacy of a word. And the (incidentally not very early) Old Testament texts linking the creation with God's word—the (first) creation narrative in the Priestly document (Gn 1:1 to 2:4a), Deutero-Isaiah and Ps 33:6—do not portray the creation as itself God's word, but rather as the word's result. *Through* God's word the heavens are made. God's speech is differentiated from its effect, which is the created work, the consequence of God's speech. God said: "Let there be," and there was.

Nevertheless we have here an assertion which is significant for our investigation. In the background is the conception that because the world is created through God's word the Logos of God dwells in the world God has created, and God's traces are imprinted in this world; so that man can discover these traces, and hence God himself, in the world. That is, the world is given to man as God's genuine communication of himself. But his communication is not issued directly in acts to the individual man, but is given for the community and made objective in the community. The word is given in the community to the individual as well; it is only in him that it comes to the fulfillment of its meaning. No matter how fond we are of conceiving of the word charismatically and dynamically, it is also and primarily an abiding, institutional reality: God's communication and challenge, discernible in the world with its pattern and order.

The "worldly" character of this word of God which is made objective in the world he has created is also confirmed even in the New Testament, the most peculiar feature of which is the revelation of the personal word of God. The appearance of the personal word of God in Jesus Christ does indeed transcend the objectification in the world of the salutation addressed by God to man. But it does not make it superfluous. Even in the New Testament order of salvation the recognition of God from creation and the moral law founded in, and recognizable from, nature retain their importance. Indeed the word which proceeds from the mouth of Christ as he teaches and challenges makes this recognition especially emphatic, brings it to its complete fulfillment, and cleanses it once more from the human limitations that it had experienced in the Old Testament "on account of the hardness of [men's] hearts" (Mt 19:8). The New Testament asserts that there is between the personal word and the world God has created as a communication of himself a relationship which confirms in a completely new way the world's character as God's communication of himself. "All things were made through the word, and without him was not anything made that was made" (Jn 1:3). The character of communication which is peculiar to creation—so that man in his worldly stewardship sees himself surrounded on every side by God's salutation—derives in the last analysis from the fact that the world was created in the personal word of God. In the incarnate Christ this word fulfills this material and worldly salutation of God to men with the personal address of the word.

Creation, animated and administered by man, now becomes history. But history becomes, under the rule of God, sacred history, the drama of redemption. In the course of time something special is added to the world's being through the fact that it is destined for man, who lives from history by making his decisions on the basis of the past and by determining history's future through his free decisions. And this special element is not yet closed by any means. On the contrary it is open for still further increase. And this further increase, which alone fulfills the meaning of history, is the drama of redemption. If history is determined by men's decisions then sacred history, the drama of redemption, is determined by the coincidence of these human decisions with God's historical planning and activity uttered in the word.

According to the Old Testament, above all Deuteronomy and Deutero-Isaiah, God's word determines history in two ways: it penetrates history and drives it onward, and it is the plan of God standing above history and yet realized in it. Thus "history also is 'the word of Yahweh,' a reality which fulfills the utterance of Yahweh. The word of history is dynamic and dianoetic: dynamic in that it accomplishes what it signifies, dianoetic in that it makes the historical process intelligible."[42] It is the very fact that the history of the Old Testament is compiled from very different sources which makes it all the more remarkable that the compilers, without planning any such result, "forged a chain of history whose links are the word of Yahweh."[43]

That man must determine history's future through his decision based on the past is not merely the discovery of modern philosophy, which expresses this fact conceptually in its distinction between chronicle and history. This is, in secular form, the same idea that the Old Testament brings out by presenting God's word in history not only as effectual, but as something audible which demands a decision. "Whereas the pre-Deuteronomic literature refers only occasionally to the connection between a *dabar* and an historical fact, the attempt is made in later stories in Deuteronomy, and above all by the Deuteronomic editor of the historical books, to show in a coherent presentation the systematic interrelation between the *dabar* and history in the whole extent of its unfolding. Yahweh's *dabar* is the nerve center of history, to which the individual events are traced back without exception. The *dabar* plays a similar role in Deutero-Isaiah and in individual psalms."[44]

But even before God's word enters into history as its effective driving power, before it becomes the word which is, so to speak, uttered in history, it is the plan which stands above the historical events, a kind of "verbum mentis" within the Godhead, according to which the word uttered in history is determined and formed. "The historical writing of Deuteronomy and of the later period . . . conceives the *dabar* also as a plan of God standing above history and possessing abiding validity; a plan which either has been realized in history or which is yet to be realized in it, and which determines history's goal. Because this divine plan aims at the people's good, God's revelation presents the promise of God which stands above history and shapes it."[45]

Here then God's word has an objective and greater-than-individual character. The individual is touched by this word as a member of history. He does not have God's word to hear directly. The word of the prophet, who receives and proclaims God's word, is valid for members of the people whose history is shaped by this word.

People, Law and Prophets

Since God's word is the power which sways and determines history it concerns the whole world he has created. It is, after all, not the chosen people alone whom God had created, but all humanity in the world he has established.

But history occurs everywhere that men shape the course of time, and therefore not only where sacred history in the narrower sense of the term occurs. Therefore God's word is a power which creates history everywhere that history exists. This is true even when we consider Christ as the center of all history. According to an ancient patristic theme the advent of the divine Logos in the world through the incarnation of Christ shines forth not only into the Old Testament, but also, as the *Logos spermaticos,* into the heathen world as well. It is quite true that the Old Testament above all is the "tutor" pointing to Christ (Gal 3:24). But even the men who, because they did not belong to the chosen people, were not under the immediate tutelage of this teacher of Christ are taken by the hand by the Logos himself in his far-reaching activity, an activity which is also at work in the wisdom of the philosophers, and which led to the incarnation of the word. Thus even history outside the people of Israel is still determined to a certain degree by the echo of God's word and tutelage, even if not directly and expressly.

But the chosen people is drawn into a dialog with God which is incomparably more intimate than this echo of God's word in the heathen world. It is precisely in this people that God's word presses history onward, and brings God's promises to fulfilment in this people. The Old Testament in speaking in the way described above of history as the objectification of God's word—which seeks to touch the individual man as an historical being—means thereby the history of the chosen people and its history alone. We know from the New Testament the reason for this exclusiveness: this people's history carries it onward toward that utterance of God's word which we know as the central and cardinal point of all history—the incarnation of the word of God in Jesus Christ.

In this connection the Old Testament presents the succession of generations from the darkness of a time completely inapprehensible in historical terms up to the period in which Israel became a people whose history under the word of God can be ascertained by the historian. And the manner of this presentation shows that the Old Testament is convinced that even the prehistoric period is directed toward the history of Israel by men to whom a word could be addressed, and to whom therefore God's word actually was addressed. God's work and his directions lead humanity's history through the darkness to the formation of the people of Israel. This striving of history toward a goal is founded precisely in the word of God, which sways history toward the people of God whom God addresses with his word and to whom he really intends to speak. In the period before Israel became a people God's word is revealed as the voice which woos this people, so to speak, and calls it forth, that God may create in it a partner to whom he can speak. Israel's history is determined then by the word of God which leads the dialog with this people and oversees its history.

Therefore what we have said above, that the individual man is touched by the word of God insofar as he is a part of sacred history, means at the same time that the individual must be a member of this people in order to be touched by God's word. The word of God is not issued anew and specifically to each individual man; rather it is issued historically. From the point at which it has touched men's history it is carried on to those who live from history and determine history by their decisions. Moreover, it is not issued separately to many isolated individuals, but socially. Because the history in which man must be directly involved is the history of a people, it follows that he must be rooted in the fellowship of this people of God. God's word speaks in history to the community of the people of Israel. It is a word addressed to the individual because it is addressed to the community of the people. The reason the word is addressed to the people however is that it may summon the individual within this fellowship to decision.

Thus God's word has in a certain sense become institutional. This people with its institutions and its life is not merely the area in which one must live in order to be able to hear God's word. Because God's word has taken shape in this people, in its history and life, the people itself is in a genuine sense the word of God. The believing Israelite, in discovering through the life of his people that he belonged to God, experienced the sending of God's word. It may strike us today as extraordinary how much political and worldly things were mixed with religious matters in the people's consciousness in the Old Testament. We now think that the two spheres must not be mixed. However we should consider whether this view, which often claims to be the only correct one, is not a makeshift solution, one preserved perhaps as the lesser evil in a world which has returned again to secularism—or which was never sufficiently won from secularism. For the Old Testament believer his is not an illegitimate mixture. To him the people to which he belongs politically is something religious. And theocracy, which was relaxed only as a concession to the monarchy (1 S 8), means that the nationally organized people with its customs, laws and explicit liturgy was the expression in which man had to receive God's communication of himself and in which he had also to discharge his devotion to God. In distinction to the church of the New Testament, membership in this people was also biologically established through the fellowship of Abraham's children. This endowed the self-consciousness of the Chosen People with a strength rooted in nature; and the transference of this attachment to the new Israel, the church, was a difficult task for Jesus and the young church.

God's word is issued in a twofold way in his Old Testament people. The two complement each other, in order to make known the special character of this God who speaks, and his manner of acting. God arouses his people through the law, contained above all in the decalogue, and in the words of the prophets to whom God's calling and mission comes again and again with ever new power. It is true that the concept "word of God" (*d'bar Yahweh*) is applied far more frequently to the prophetic word than to the law. Nevertheless the statement that the provisions of the law given through Moses are the *d'brim Yahweh* (the words of God) is so clear, not to mention frequent, as to make it impossible for us to interpret even the law otherwise than as God's word. The above term occurs in the singular two hundred and forty-one times, and of these the meaning in two hundred and twenty-five passages is identical. The term is applied so often to the prophetic word that "the word of God is almost everywhere the *terminus technicus* for prophetical revelation in words."[46] When applied to the law the notion of God's word occurs more frequently in the plural. This is easy to explain, since the law contained of course a multiplicity of individual provisions, which consequently appear to be many words of God.

The history of the Old Testament people of God is permeated with the conviction that this people, in receiving its law and thus its unity and existence from God himself on Mount Sinai, has become, through the fact that God has addressed it, *the* people of God in distinction to all other peoples (who are in fact not people at all, but "no-peoples"). When he received the law for the people "Moses came and told the people all the words of the Lord and all the ordinances; and all the people answered with one voice, and said: 'All the words which the Lord has spoken we will do.' And Moses wrote all the words of the Lord . . ." (Ex 24:3f). And when Moses repeats the ten commandments before the people and reminds them that this law has been given by God he says: "I stood between the Lord and you at that time, to declare to you the word of the Lord" (Dt 5:5). And this "word of the Lord" is then proclaimed anew: it is the decalogue, the heart of the law.

Conduct in accordance with the law is therefore also understood as conduct in accordance with God's word. "The person who does anything with a high hand . . . shall be cut off from among his people. Because he has despised the word of the Lord . . ." (Nm 15:30f). When the book of the law is rediscovered it is recognized: ". . . great is the wrath of the Lord that is poured out on us, because our fathers have not kept the word of the Lord, to do according to all that is written in this book" (2 Chr 34:21b).

Here is testimony from the other side of the distinction between the biblical understanding of God's word and the Greek conception of the Logos. When God utters his word it does not have academic significance, and is not a purely objective communication of things which could not be known without this word. On the contrary God's word is always demand, commandment, law, even in those passages where it seems at first to communicate theologically important truths and perceptions. Even when God speaks about his own being and essence and that of his creation he is still voicing a demand. What he demands is man's submission. One does not enter the luminous realm of divine knowledge without having to draw the conclusions of such knowledge for life and conduct.

It becomes clear here, if anywhere, how strongly God's word seeks to assume concrete form. It may be that some people who are impressed with a conception of God full of dynamism and power are disinclined to conceive of the word of this living God as being something static. Nor will they be disposed to see his word bound up in the national and institutional order of a people's life. What we shall have to say in a moment about the prophetic word of God will appear to confirm this disinclination. But nevertheless it is undeniable that the word of God already in the Old Testament, but also in the New Testament, is presented as also bound up with an institution.

In distinction to the word of the law which outlasts all the individual situations of the people's life and is intended to be realized in each of them, the word of the prophets is bound up with specific situations. The content of the prophetic word spoken here and now makes concrete in a temporally fixed individual situation the plan and will of God, which are contained in the law in a form transcending temporal limitations. That is the reason why the prophetic word of God is not issued in the first place in written form. The word of the prophet is written only later, to proclaim to succeeding generations God's intervention in the stages of his people's life. For when God intervenes in the history of his people through the work of the prophets he demands from the following generations as well that they remember in faith what he has done and make their own decisions in obedience to him. But the word of the prophet has gone forth as God's word long before it was written down. And before being written as a part of holy scripture it has been recalled many times over in the living tradition of the people. But just for this reason the prophetic utterance takes written form as well, so that later generations can see, by reference to this record, whether and how far their people has followed the prophetic word of God. This occurs not that the people may judge its own forefathers, but rather that it may draw consequences for itself, to correct, where correction is needed, and to follow the lessons of the past where they appear as warnings for similar situations. The historical situation in which God has spoken through his prophets is of course never so unique that it cannot afford instruction for later times.

Now it is no coincidence that God's word is issued in this double form, through the law and through the prophets. The two supplement each other, testify to each from a special viewpoint of God's revelation of himself in the history of his people. In the form of the permanent, ever-abiding law the eternal unchanging God summons men from their ephemerality and transience, from their prepossession with momentary needs and joys, to take a genuine share already in this world in his eternity. For the man of the Old Testament, who hardly knew anything as yet of a genuine and inalienable participation in God's eternity as the goal of human existence, it was all the more important that God's word should at least give him some idea that he was summoned from an eternity which transcended everything transitory and temporary. In giving his word in the law God testifies that he is the eternal one, the "ancient of days" (Dn 6:13).

But God acts from eternity very dynamically, often breaking suddenly into the history of his people. If the permanency of the law easily tempts men to oppose their own arbitrary action to the law's supposed rigidity, God proceeds against this willfulness in the dynamic form of his word, for the proclamation of which he calls the prophets and sends them forth. It is true that its punitive provisions already protect the law, which is given once and for all, from the unhindered ravages of men of evil will. When despite these provisions man in his arbitrary self-will seeks to lay violent hands on the law's divine word, the prophetic word of warning recalls the law's urgency, threatens punishments against him who refuses to fulfill the law, and sets forth the connection between the events of history and men's decisions for right and wrong—thus showing again and again how active is the presence of God in the word he has given to his people in the law. The law is intended to be heard and observed today (Dt 4:40; 5:3; 11:26–8). It possesses therefore a powerful dynamism which is made explicit through the word of the prophets.

According to the understanding of the Old Testament however the law has in itself a genuine prophetic character as well. And this is fulfilled and made real by the ever-fresh word of the prophets. The law is understood not so much as a codified collection of regulations, but rather as wisdom for life which penetrates the whole of man's existence. This wisdom determines the life of the member of God's people because it keeps his life within the divine covenant. The law is the record of God's wisdom which dwells in Israel and which makes the law the book of the covenant of the Most High (Sir 24:18–31). It is true that factors of a very natural, economic, geographic, social and historical kind have also contributed concretely and in fact to the development of the Old Testament law. "But these elements which determined the actual life of the people of Israel were always considered in the biblical writings as the expression of God's leadership: as the words of God, or as his torah."[47]

Therefore we must not misunderstand the dynamics of the word, as if the word simply dropped unpredictably and arbitrarily into the personal life of the individual man in order to withdraw him from the bond to the community which is established by the law. The word of God speaks in the law to the individual as a member of the people. This word of wisdom issued in the past has received in the codex of the law a permanent form transcending history; and on this basis it seeks to reach men afresh in every age and to speak to them. The word of God is near at hand in the law, so that it is not necessary first to fetch it down from heaven, or from beyond the sea. On the contrary it is possible to have it in one's own mouth and heart (Dt 30:14). And this demand of God's word in the law to be heard here and now is insisted upon again and again in the words of the prophets. What the prophet says is never opposed to the law, but serves its realization. For God's word cannot contradict itself. Even when the dynamism of God's word comes out most strongly, namely in the charismatic conception of the word which we find in the prophets, the bond with the institution is not relinquished. Of course there is also in the Old Testament a tension between the prophetic and charismatic elements and the institutional element. We find this often. But the word of God in the prophets remains bound to the people, its history and its law. This word too touches the individual through the fellowship of the people. The word of the prophet also finds its norm in the divine word of the law. The harmony of the prophet's word with the word of the law is precisely the criterion of its authenticity. "If a prophet arises among you, or a dreamer of dreams, and gives you a sign or a wonder, and the sign or wonder which he tells you comes to pass, and if he says, 'Let us go after other gods, which you have not known, and let us serve them,' you shall not listen to the words of that prophet or to that dreamer of dreams; for the Lord your God is testing you, to know whether you love the Lord your God with all your heart and with all your soul. You shall walk after the Lord your God and fear him, and keep his commandments and obey his voice, and you shall serve him and cleave to him" (Dt 13:1–4).

2 God's Word in the Church

What has been said about the word in the pre-ecclesiastical realm of the Old Testament was not intended as an historical description of a past affair without any present significance. What came into being then in consequence of God's plan and command has already helped to determine the form of God's word today. For the church, in which alone the word of God is validly preserved and effectually proclaimed, knows itself to be the fulfillment of the Old Testament redemptive fellowship. Therefore if God's word has determined the history of the Old Testament people of God it must have retained this role in the church of the New Testament. And anyone who wishes to understand the church Christ founded must look first at its Old Testament foundation. It is true that the books of the Old Testament do not have for the Christian of the new covenant exactly the same meaning the words of these books had for the Old Testament Israelite. The Christian reads the Old Testament as a word and a report which await their fulfillment in Christ, and which can be understood in their proper sense only in the light of this fulfillment. But it is just here that the Old Testament has its significance for our understanding of the Christian life. The Christian life can be understood only if we do not overlook the fact that this life transcends and surpasses in its demands not only every purely natural human life, but even the Old Testament. This transcendence also invalidates a number of things. Thus the New Testament Christian cannot adopt the imprecatory psalms of the Old Testament, for instance, and pray them in their literal and direct sense, as the Israelite of the old covenant did. In the offices of the New Testament church the Christian worshiper cannot use the words of these psalms to call down evil on his human enemies in the same sense in which the man of the Old Testament did. The New Testament worshiper will be able to deal with such words of prayer only by remaining conscious as he reads them of how far beyond the Old Testament attitude he, as a man of the New Testament, is led by the teaching and grace of Christ. And this should remind him not only of how great a gift is given him through redemption and grace, but also of the greatness of the obligation they impose.

It is impossible therefore simply to transfer unexamined everything which was true of the Old Testament redemptive community to the church of the New Testament as if it all found its development and fulfillment there. It is necessary to see what has been dropped in Christ's church, and what, on the other hand, has been fulfilled. Here however God's personal communication of himself in his word belongs not to the things which have been dropped, but to those which have been fulfilled. The fulfillment of the New Testament church consists of course precisely in the fact that "God, who in many and various ways spoke of old to our fathers by the prophets, has in these last days spoken to us by a Son, whom he appointed the heir of all things, through whom also he created the world" (Heb 1:1). Thus the pre-Christian utterance of God's word came to fulfillment in the church. Conversely there is in the continuing life of the church no further new word of divine revelation. The reason is not that the church has to live by God's word to any lesser degree than the Old Testament people of God. But in Christ God's word has been spoken in such a manner that no further utterance is needed, but only further development and explanation, and above all life on the basis of this word.

The Church as the Word of God

Works of art are generally displayed in a frame befitting their value. Precious stones are given a setting, the form and value of which alone show the value of the stone. And man applies this general law of style to himself as well. He expresses the value he attaches to himself by clothing his body not with just any kind of garment that is sufficient for the demands of warmth and decency: rather through well tailored and groomed clothes he gives his body a frame which shows its value, one perhaps which even raises its value. Such a frame belongs so completely to the content itself that the whole is sometimes referred to along with the name of the content, sometimes with that of its setting.

Even when we speak of God's word in the church we have fixed our gaze upon the word in which God imparts himself to men in redeeming grace. The word is the valuable content, the church the setting. And here too the two are described somtimes in terms of the content, somtimes in terms of the setting. Still it is in each case the two together which we have in mind. Whoever, aware of the context, speaks of God's word must mean this word insofar as it comes to men through the church. And whoever speaks of the church means the New Testament people of God as the redemptive community touched by God's word. Such a fluctuating terminology has a special justification in the fact that the church not only itself contains God's word but also appears before men as itself the word of God. Therefore Paul testifies to the Christians of Thessalonica: "You became imitators of us and of the Lord, for you received the word in much affliction, with joy inspired by the Holy Spirit; so that you became an example to all believers in Macedonia and in Achaia. For not only has the word of the Lord sounded forth from you in Macedonia and Achaia, but your faith in God has gone forth everywhere, so that we need not say anything" (1 Th 1:6–8).

When the church appears in the New Testament as the body of Christ this is of course intended to characterize directly the mystical unity of the visible and social church with its divine-human Head, the exalted Lord who through his Holy Spirit quickens the church as a living supernatural organism. In actual fact however this conception points also to the kinship of the Lord's mystical body with his individual, physical body. This kinship consists in the fact that in the church, in a manner similar to that which obtains in the case of the Lord's individual body, the invisible God presents himself in visible form to the disciples and the people. The relationship of body and soul means more than that the body is the vessel, the covering or the instrument of the soul. The soul expresses itself in the body as well; the soul's secrets are manifested in the body, consciously or unconsciously, through a free act or because betrayed through an involuntary sign. But now we may, like Leo XII[48] and, with reference to him, Pius XII,[49] call the Holy Spirit the soul of the Lord's mystical body, the church.

In a passage in the tenth chapter of the first epistle to the Corinthians Paul speaks of the body of Christ in a manner which clarifies the entire perspective and character of this notion, as well as its application to Christ and his church. Referring to the mystery of the eucharist he says: "The bread that we break, is it not the fellowship in the body of Christ?" (1 Cor 10:16). What kind of a body of Christ is it then, the fellowship of which is signified and conveyed by the mystery of the bread in the eucharist? Is it the physical, individual body of Christ—now raised to heaven, it is true, but which still remains the same body that the disciples "saw with their eyes, looked upon and touched with their hands" (1 Jn 1:1)? Or is it Christ's eucharistic body, the species of bread, which contains our Lord's individual body, invisibly, hidden, but still truly present? Or is it, finally, our Lord's mystical body, the church, the unity of which Paul warns his readers to maintain? In fact it is all three modes of Christ's body which are meant. The passage speaks directly of eating Christ's body as contained under the sacramental species of bread. But this eating has its importance and power from the fact that our Lord's own individual body which the disciples saw and touched is present in this food and receives him who partakes thereof into the fellowship of his life, and allows him to share in that sacrificial devotion to the Father which culminates in the risen life. This sacramental eating however is a meal of fellowship that displays the church as the mystical body of Christ which is continually edified and fulfilled in the reception of the sacramental body of its Lord.

These three realities can all be designated with the same name, the body of Christ, only because there is something to be found in each of them which in fact characterizes our Lord's body. This is—if not alone then still chiefly—that in all three a this-worldly, visible reality bears witness to an invisible, divine reality and makes it present, just as vividly and truly as the body bears witness to the soul and makes it present. And thus through contact with this visible element one comes into living contact with the divine foundation of its existence. With regard to Christ's physical, individual body we know that "He who sees me sees the Father" (Jn 14:9). With regard to the eucharistic bread we read: "This *is* my body" (Mt 26:26 and parallel passages). And Paul speaks of the church as "his body which is the church" (Col 1:24). In all three modes of bodily existence therefore we see, touch, eat and live that divine reality which lives in and through the man Jesus Christ. In all three instances Paul's statement, made concerning Christ in his bodily form, is true: he is "the image of the invisible God" (Col 1:15). Thus God utters himself here in the visible human realm and communicates himself to men in a manner which human words could indeed aim at, but which they could never attain. In Jesus Christ the living kindness of God has "appeared," has achieved its "epiphany" (Tit 3:4). And if the church is Christ's body with that degree of realism which Paul obviously intended, then the portrayal of God in the church, his appearance and self-utterance which occurred once in the incarnate Christ, is to a certain degree broadened and continued. Christ is God's word to men because in him the second divine person has taken human form and a bodily nature. So the church, because and insofar as it is Christ's body, is in at least a similar manner God's word to men in the world.

The church is God's word in a manner similarly direct, though not quite as direct, as Christ himself is God's word. And more than that, the church is not simply in the same manner the word of God as the actual preaching of God's word which takes place in the church. But this limitation on both sides does not constitute too great a qualification of the statement that the church can really be considered God's word to men.

The mystical body of the God-man can be compared with him as the word of God because he does not utter his word in a passing act, but presents it in permanent form. It is true that Christ also proclaimed the words of God, and the church communicates these words in its preaching. But already before these words are proclaimed both Christ and the church are the word of God. Both the individual and the "ecclesiastical" Christ are therefore the word in the sense of a sign which proclaims the reality it signifies by its very presence, and not by being uttered. The First Vatican Council, adopting the words of the prophet Isaiah, has called the church "the sign raised among the nations" (Is 11:12).[50] This sign is not intended to draw attention merely to the fact that God has opened himself to men. Certainly Vatican I means to call the church a sign in this sense as well. In order to have a rational foundation for his faith and to be morally responsible for it man needs signs which guarantee him certain premises of that faith. In order to accept as true what God has revealed because the revelation comes from God it must first be established that God has in fact revealed something. And this fact must be established with the authority of valid testimony. In order to supply these preliminary conditions to the actual act of faith God asserts himself through signs in every way which can direct man's glance beyond the realm of his human, worldly and natural powers and open his perception for the word which God communicates to man in revelation. The Vatican Council reckons the church itself among these signs. "Indeed the church is in itself a great and abiding motive of credibility and a sign of its divine sending which cannot be gainsaid; and this in virtue of its remarkable dissemination, its outstanding holiness, and inexhaustible fruitfulness in everything which is good, and because of its catholic unity and invincible stability. Thus it comes about that this church, like a sign raised among the nations, invites to itself those who do not yet believe, while making its own children the more certain that the faith which they profess rests upon the surest of foundations."[51]

But this significance does not yet bring the sign into actual kinship with the word. For here the church appears more as the work which, in its origin, its continuance, its properties and efficacy, cannot be explained by human powers and which leads men through this miraculous character to infer an other-worldly, indeed a divine author. Seen in this light the same is also true of the church (as we have found earlier to be true) with regard to work in distinction to the word. The church is certainly also a means by which God expresses himself. But it is not actually that "*medium in quo*" which itself contains and makes known in substance what God intends to express. Rather the church is the "*medium ex quo,*" a statement on the basis of which it is possible to infer new knowledge—though, to be sure, this inference is more immediate than the inference we make of the creator on the basis of the created world. The church, like every miraculous sign, is an indication that God is at work.

In the gospels however the miracles Christ performed are not called signs because they awake astonishment in man and so dispose him to recognize a divine cause. The New Testament realizes that Christ's miraculous signs are intended rather to convey a content as well: they appear, that is, as statements too, as a word. The miraculous multiplication of the loaves is not intended merely to show that God in his authority stands behind him who performs this miracle and confirms his utterance. It is also itself an utterance in a certain sense: saying that Christ is the true bread for hungry man. The miracle at the marriage in Cana is performed not merely as a sign on the basis of which one can infer that God is somehow at work. It is a sign which says something. And as such it points like a word to a higher marriage in comparison with which this human marriage becomes rather unimportant. The miracles of healing and his raisings of the dead are performed by our Lord as signs which reveal something through what they contain: Christ is the savior for men's real sickness; he raises men from the worst death, sin, to the very life of God himself which is given to men that they may share it.

The same is also true therefore of the church Christ has set up as a sign among the nations. The church is in its existence, its stability and its character first of all a work which can be explained only through God's miraculous power. This sign is intended to point men to the credibility of the church's message. Seen in this light, as the sign of its credibility which is guaranteed by God, the church is not the same as the content of the message it has to proclaim. The church so conceived would still not be really a word, not yet the bearer of a real content communicated by God. But in fact, to a certain degree, the church is this also. It is not the bare fact of the church's existence which points man, as he considers the causality here, to a super-worldly and superhuman author. The character of the church's existence, what it is, expresses a content which is in a genuine sense a divine communication and a revelation.

This conception of the church finds expression in the ancient tradition that membership in the church is the visible portrayal of, and thus the expression of membership in, the living fellowship with God in grace which is God's kingdom. This is shown with special clarity in early Christian penitential practice. The sinner is excluded from the living fellowship of the eucharist in the church. This makes visible the separation from God which has occurred through sin. The peace with the church which is won again through penance brings about the regaining of peace with God and makes this peace sacramentally visible.[52]

Thus it is possible to call the church itself God's word to men in an analogous sense. In the church God expresses symbolically before men his redemptive purpose and the realization of this purpose in his kingdom. The fellowship of the church, penetrated by God's Spirit and disposed in a social form, expresses God's saving intention for men. The church is the sign of this intention to save. And this sign does not merely show *that* God wants to do something here. It expresses rather *what* he wants to do for men.

We can therefore compare Christ's mystical body with

Christ himself. As a result of the hypostatic union his human nature imparts to the word of God within the Godhead human visibility and tangibility, as the audible word makes its intended meaning visible and tangible. It is true that this comparison is weakened by the fact that the church is not hypostatically united with God's Son; but this fact does not invalidate the comparison. This objection is to be found from time to time in Protestant authors who criticize the Catholic conception of the mystery of the church: "The most profound and damaging confusion of the message of the incarnation does not occur outside in the world. . . . It occurs within, in Christendom, in the doctrinal teaching of the church itself. . . . What does this confusion consist of? It arises from the church's own view and description of itself as the continuation of God's incarnation in Christ. This confusion has entered . . . into the fundamental understanding which the Roman Catholic Church has of itself, and is maintained and defended there with complete openness."[53] It would of course be a gross misunderstanding of the nature of the church to attempt to conceive of it as an expression and utterance of God as direct as Christ's human nature, which is hypostatically united with God's word. Despite the great difference however the comparison is justified. The visible church is penetrated by God to such a degree that a certain analogy does exist with Christ's human nature, which in turn is penetrated by God's Logos. In any case the tradition of the church fathers considered this parallel justified. That the parallel can also be wrongly understood is of course indisputable. Even a statement of the so-called Athanasian creed from the fourth century is open to such a misunderstanding. The statement concerns the unity of the human and divine natures in Christ: "As the reasonable soul and body are but one man, so also is God and man but one Christ."[54] How easy it is to misunderstand this phrase, as if God and man were two incomplete substances which are combined in Christ to constitute a living total substance. Despite this danger the comparison drawn in this creed does say something important about the living unity of the two natures in the one person of the Logos. A similar misunderstanding can also arise when the church is compared with the God-man. Nevertheless the comparison is not therefore simply unjustified. As in this sentence of the Athanasian creed the divine Logos in the God-man is compared with the soul in the human body, so is it also possible in accordance with the evidence of what happened on Pentecost to compare God's Spirit in the church with the soul in the human body.

But this comparison then gives to the visible church the character of God's word, one similar to that possessed by Christ in his bodily existence. In the church God makes himself visible and audible; he utters himself in the church. At the epiphany the invisible God manifested himself to men through Jesus Christ. And this manifestation continues to be accomplished in a certain sense in the church which, as the visible form of God's kingdom, makes God's presence in the world visible.

Hence it comes about that the church must carry out the ministry of proclaiming God's word, which belongs to it by nature, by proclaiming itself as well. It is not that the church is itself the ultimate and actual goal of its redemptive ministry of the word: but the church is to a certain extent the super-temporal, authorized figure of God's word which is at work in each individual act of preaching; moreover it is through preaching that men's connection with the church is established. And because the church is not a mere functionary performing an external service, as are societies and institutions organized with a purely worldly purpose, but portrays tangibly in its social form the living fellowship with

God and makes this fellowship present in this world, the gathering of men into the church's living union means the corporal realization of salvation itself.

The redemptive encounter with God is a kind of dialog. But in such a dialog the two partners meet each other in the word which, so to speak, stands between them. One has uttered the word; the other, by hearing the word and receiving it, meets there him who has communicated himself in this word. Thus the church stands as the word of the Lord between God and men in this world. God communicates himself to men in this mystical body of his son as he also did in the incarnate Christ. Man must receive the church as God's word by himself being received into the church. This is the mystery of the church, which as Christ's body shares in the verbal character of Christ himself.

The Biblical Word in the Church

The church, itself God's word to the world, also possesses God's word as a gift she must pass on to men through her preaching. The church must make sure that the word of God entrusted to it from the time of the apostles resounds. But if this is the case then it must be possible to find God's word somewhere or other in the church's life, and prior to its preaching activity and distinct from the church itself. God's word must be something that can be taken and passed on, a gift which is present like a concrete thing and not something which must first be created by the church's activity. But what is this something and what does it look like, this thing on which the church must perform its "ministry of the word"?

What the church has to pass on to men in its preaching is without question what God has revealed to men. And this divine revelation entrusted to the church to be proclaimed has just as unquestionably its climax and culmination in Jesus Christ, with whose entrance into our history the kingdom of God has come upon us (Mt 12:28; Lk 11:20), and with it judgment (Jn 12:31 and 48; Mt 11:20–4), forgiveness (Mk 2:1–12) and God's presence (Jn 10:30 and 38; Mt 11:25f). Christ is the I AM in the fullest sense (Jn 8:58; 10; 11:25). So it is Christ as *the* word of God who is the actual object of the church's preaching. But the gospel of Jesus Christ entered into the hearing church from the mouth of Jesus Christ through apostles who first of all listen, as disciples, and who then speak in Christ's stead (2 Cor 5:20). The church of the post-apostolic age has not received any other task than that of continually proclaiming to men this word of God which the apostles received and passed on to the church. This living proclamation and the equally living hearing of the community is the apostolic tradition, so called because it passes on what has been received from the apostles. Moreover it expands through development the explicit preaching of the apostles for the simple reason that this passing on of the preaching in the living history of tradition "under the suggestion of the Holy Spirit"[55] gradually brings to light all the original depths of the word of revelation.

At the point of the transition from the period of the apostolic tradition to the post-apostolic church which lives from this tradition—and we must not take the word "point" too literally here, since we are speaking of the boundary of this transition more in principle than in a temporal sense—at this point we must insert yet another link which must not be overlooked. The apostolic message of the living church in its first beginnings does not pass over invisibly and inobstrusively into the tradition of the post-apostolic time. There is an objective, "real" form of God's word which is transmitted to the church's tradition as the record of the apostolic message. And this link which serves both to join and to separate the "normative" preaching of the apostles and the preaching of the post-apostolic church for which it is the norm is holy scripture. The sure divine inspiration which is part of the church's deposit of faith gives to scripture a position in the church's life and faith, as well as in its tradition and preaching, which is not achieved by any other kind of word. Scripture must therefore be preserved in its special position without impairing for the faith of the individual Christian the normative importance of the church's living tradition with its own special characteristics.

Catholic theology still has in this question a broad area for further clarification. The Council of Trent did not speak unequivocally about this matter. Its formulation leaves aside a decision about the relationship of scripture and tradition.[56] In our own time a discussion of this question has also arisen.[57] The "and" with which the Council of Trent links scripture and tradition as sources of faith—the revealed "faith and order is contained in written books and unwritten traditions"[58]—is by no means unambiguous. This formulation permits three different conceptions of the relationship between scripture and the church's doctrinal preaching which hands on the tradition.

This "and" could be interpreted in the sense of "partly . . . partly." Thus one part of the deposit of faith would come to us in holy scripture and the other in the living tradition—which would thus, in a sense, supplement scripture. Therefore we find from time to time that the bible and tradition are placed side by side, without much reflection, as two sources for our knowledge of revelation. In this case however tradition would have a double task. First of all it would have to transmit and also interpret scripture and unfold its meaning. But at the same time it would have to transmit a deposit of faith that had—just as much as holy scripture—been received by the apostles, but which was handed down separately from the biblical record. The church's preaching would have to supplement holy scripture through a divine revelation received and transmitted independently of scripture.

A second possibility for the interpretation of the Council of Trent's "and" is to translate it "both . . . and." This would mean that the two sources, holy scripture and tradition, each contained God's entire revelation. This conception differs from a third possibility we shall present in a moment in that in this case scripture and tradition stand side by side without any particular relationship to one another. This would leave the individual free to choose from which of these two sources he wishes to draw his faith. This view, with the implication that the two sources simply exist side by side without any particular relationship with one another, is probably not represented in catholic theology. However a third manner of understanding Trent's "and" has come to the fore recently which is actually a strengthening of this second view.

According to this view scripture and tradition are seen as joined more or less in the sense expressed by the word "with." Holy scripture together with the living tradition offers God's revelation to the faithful. In this view the deposit of faith revealed by God is presented through holy scripture insofar as it is communicated and interpreted by the church's tradition under the guidance of the Holy Spirit. But the same thing can just as well be said conversely: God's revelation is transmitted to us through the living tradition, insofar as it bears holy scripture in its hands and brings to light from the depths of scripture what God's inspiring Spirit has hidden there. What tradition has to transmit to later generations, to interpret and to bring to light, is precisely holy scripture and scripture alone. For holy scripture is formally God's word and constitutes the substance of the church's activity in its tradition and preaching. For in scripture God's word is transmitted in its objective form to the faithful hands of the church, which must then interpret, unfold and apply this word in its preaching. Scripture and tradition are not the same, nor are they two independent sources. Rather they are bound together in organic unity.

It is J. R. Geiselmann above all who has reintroduced this concept into the theological discussion; his interest in the matter followed upon his researches into the Catholic Tübingen school of the previous century.[59] And Father J. Beumer S.J. has demonstrated that there is a "Catholic principle of scripture" which is based upon ancient tradition, and that "at the beginning of scholastic theology and long after its climactic period the bible was the regular text for theological lectures."[60] The textbooks of systematic theology were called "*Sententiae divinae pagina,*" and the science of theology is actually called "*sacra pagina.*"[61]

Thus holy scripture stands at the beginning of the post-apostolic tradition, as Jesus Christ himself stood at the beginning of the apostolic preaching. And when the church today traces its preaching and dogmatic decisions back explicitly to holy scripture even in those cases where it is impossible for those who look at these things purely philologically to follow the church's line of reasoning—as, for instance, in the case of the last two marian dogmas—this is done only in part to supply a justifying proof. For the other part, and this is far more important, the church does this in order to confess that it preaches not its own word but the word of God which Jesus Christ has transmitted to his church. The church's preaching interprets holy scripture under the leadership of the Holy Spirit, who permeates the church's life and who alone can bring up from the depths everything which he has in his inspiration laid down and intended in the word of holy scripture.

The question of the interpretation of this "and" which joins the bible and the preaching tradition is not without relevance for an understanding of the church's proclamation of the word of God. For if bible and tradition existed side by side as two partial sources, there would be in the ministry of the word another task alongside and independent of the interpretation and proclamation of holy scripture, to which the word which this task serves would not be entrusted so objectively and tangibly, and therefore without the same symbolic power either. But when this "and" joins holy scripture as an integral vessel of revelation, tradition being understood as the church's faith which lives from scripture, then the ministry of the word that the church must perform consists precisely in transmitting holy scripture and in drawing out from its depths the whole meaning put there by God's Spirit.

Moreover the differences of opinion we have mentioned actually affect our subject only when we ask where the church is to find what it must proclaim to men as the content of God's word. However we interpret the relationship between scripture and tradition it remains true that tradition communicates only the content of God's word, that is, that it is God's word only in the material sense, whereas holy scripture is, in virtue of divine inspiration, itself formally God's word. It is necessary though, in considering holy scripture as the word of God, to avoid two erroneous extremes: "On the one hand the error, similar to Monophysitism in christology, which blends the word of scripture and the word of God completely; . . . and on the other hand the more Nestorian error which considers the word of scripture and the word of God as existing side by side in a purely external relationship. The proper mean . . . is observed by every theology of scripture which—like Catholic theology—recognizes God himself as the actual author and the existing word of scripture as formally his word, but which respects the human author as an instrument whose mental capacities are used to the full, and which considers his humanly uttered word as something which mediates revelation and as testimony effected by God. Holy scripture is indeed God's word formally, but not immediately. This is the prerogative of the Logos alone. . . . Because God has taken this word unto himself in a unique way which is not to be found so completely anywhere else, scripture alone is formally and in the strictest sense God's word."[62] Thus the priority of scripture over tradition becomes visible. And it must be respected. In its preaching the church has to communicate what God has spoken as his word. But holy scripture is the word of God and hence the object of that proclamation which is tradition, and of that tradition which consists in proclamation. Scripture contains God's utterance in the verbal receptacle he has fashioned through his revelation. God's utterance, thus written down once and for all, outlasts all ages. Holy scripture "is the word of God insofar as it mediates God's word (through the human nature of the Logos and those who are witnesses to him), brings it to man and confronts him with it."[63]

It is therefore disputable whether the content of divine revelation has come down to later generations in holy scripture, since it is contained fully and completely in scripture, or whether it has come down in part alongside scripture through purely oral tradition. But there can be no disputing the fact that holy scripture, in distinction to the church's preaching and tradition, *is* the word of God formally, whereas the preaching and tradition of the church transmit God's word in the material and substantial sense. God's special work of inspiration has laid down his revelation in the bible as in a permanent verbal receptacle. Holy scripture is not merely a report of something God communicated at some earlier date in word and work. It is that as well. But this report is given by God himself, and in the making of this report there is a further and new self-communication of God as the revealing giver of salvation. He himself bears witness to the manner in which he has communicated himself to men in the Old Testament drama of redemption and in the formation of the church of the new covenant.

It may perhaps also be disputed whether and how far the bible, in view of its manner of writing history and the intention of its presentation, portrays the historical events of the Old Testament history, of the life of Jesus and of the young church in all respects as they actually "happened." But it cannot be disputed that these events are at any rate found in the bible in the manner in which God has fixed them in his word and in which he presents them to us for our decision. In the word of the bible we meet God as he testifies to his redemptive activity in history. And this is more decisive than the certainty that we have before our eyes a chronicle which is objective and exact in every individual feature. We are intended to encounter God as he communicates his saving power in history. Even more important than what is reported is the God who reports. He it is whom we receive in his word when we ponder holy scripture in faith.

In this formal sense we meet God's word only in holy scripture. For all other ways in which God's word has been issued were bound to the moment and have faded away. The word also passes away with the breath that has spoken it. It attains permanency only if it is written down, as was the case with the bible. When the believer reads holy scripture he does not merely receive the content of divine revelation, as occurs when he hears and receives the church's preaching of its faith. Rather he receives in holy scripture the meaning and the word, the content and the vessel God has formed for it, what has been spoken and God's speech. Hence the reading and meditation of holy scripture is important not only because of the content we discover there, but also because of the organ through which this content is presented: the word in which God presents himself.

Therefore we may certainly say that the scales have now turned very considerably in favor of the view that holy scripture contains the entire content of revelation. This content is, to be sure, in many respects undeveloped and hidden. And this view presents the oral tradition with the task of bringing the content more to light and to explicit development in the course of time. For why should this formal word of God exist in the church if not to enkindle the church's whole life of faith and to set in motion that proclamation by which the word is transmitted? If holy scripture is, formally considered, the only mode of existence which God's word has in the church, should we not then assume that in the efforts made in behalf of this verbal receptacle of God's revelation the entire content of this revelation is unfolded for the faith of the church?

3 The Ministry of the Word

We must now turn our attention to several New Testament texts which refer very insistently to the importance for the church of hearing the word of God. One such passage (Mk 3:31) reports that our Lord is about to proclaim the word of God when it is reported to him that his mother and brethren wish to speak with him. Who would not expect that respect and love would have caused the Son to dismiss the listening group and devote himself to his mother? But his mother seems to be entirely unimportant to him. Our Lord refers beyond her to all those who hear the word of

God and heed it. He returns a similar answer to the praise addressed to him by a woman in the crowd, but the answer is directed at his mother (Lk 11:27). Here too our Lord does not seem to join in this woman's praise or confirm it. Here too we have the impression that he wants to look away from Mary. Or more correctly he seems to want to direct his gaze beyond her or through her to all those who are blessed because they hear the word of God and keep it.

It is not legitimate to use these texts in arguing against Catholic veneration of Mary. On the contrary they can be interpreted as the foundation and confirmation of the Catholic belief in Mary, through which the veneration of our Lady achieves at the same time its actual depth. These passages cannot mean that Mary is not entitled to the reverence and veneration of believing Christendom. Such an allegation would be contradicted not only by the common ancient practice of the church but also by the biblical prophecy: "From henceforth all generations will call me blessed" (Lk 1:48). It is true however that in these passages Mary is freed from an isolated consideration and shown in a transparency which gives her a new significance and serves as a warning that marian veneration must not go beyond its true purpose. When our Lord refers to those who hear the word of God and keep it then Mary is not excluded from this statement but rather included, since she is the original image of this community of hearers. The fellowship of those who by hearing and receiving the word of God become partakers of redemption has found in Mary a personal figure and representation.

This observation is no less important for the correct view of the church than it is for the veneration of Mary. For the church is the community of those who hear the word of God and keep it.

The Church as a Community of Hearers

As such the church is a reality in this world which has its gaze directed to the other world. The church, considered as a body which listens, is the bride who hears from her bridegroom the loving word of revelation and in this word receives the bridegroom himself. The church's bridegroom is the glorified Lord who through his Holy Spirit communicates himself and his life to the church in this world. In one sense the church is an eschatological reality. For although it exists in this world the church receives its actual life from the other world where its exalted bridegroom and Lord is. This leads at once to another sense in which the church is an eschatological reality, namely that its this-worldly existence is intended to find its fulfillment in union with the bridegroom, and in future participation in his royal glory. The church lives as a community of hearers in two dimensions, since the word of the Lord comes from on high but is proclaimed in the horizontal dimension of the visible church in this world.

The church takes its being from the hearing of the word. And this word summons the church not only from the nations of the gentiles but also, as the fate of Jesus and his disciples makes more and more clear, out of the narrow-minded Old Testament people of God. The church begins to attain its fullness of being when God's word in its full form enters into the history of this world. The word of God becomes man in Jesus Christ. The church begins with Mary, his mother, as the original hearer. She received from God's messenger the word which he brought, and answered it with the statement: "I am the handmaid of the Lord; be it done unto me according to your word" (Lk 1:38). In Mary's decision the decision of the listening community was realized in the form of a type and God's word was granted entrance into our history. The disciples of Jesus accepted Mary's word. They hear, not always with immediate understanding, and not always very willingly. But they do allow themselves in their encounter with the word which came from the mouth of their master to be aroused to readiness and acceptance. And this is the crucial difference between the behavior of the disciples and that of the mass. And it is quite remarkable how even Jesus' attitude toward the mass of the people differs from his attitude toward the little band of disciples. Our Lord expressed himself quite indignantly with regard to the incomprehension of the crowds and applies to them the words of the prophet about the eyes that do not see and the ears that do not hear. But our Lord's anger does not fall upon the disciples. Why not actually? They have certainly not understood much more, as their question shows. But they ask so that they may be led to an understanding of what our Lord means. Whereas the broad mass does not bother any further about the word they have not understood, the disciples strive to understand it. They are concerned about the Lord's word. They want to hear it with that hearing which is more than acoustic reception (Mt 13:1–16). Here is the church's life of faith developing in the alternation of proclamation and hearing, questioning or misunderstanding and more profound proclamation. The community of hearers does not need to understand everything at first hearing. There is much that it will never understand completely. But in its reception of God's word this community must enter into dialog with God and penetrate into the depths of his word. Only here does the church achieve its existence as the community of those who hear the word of God in order to keep it, and keep it in order that they may be able better to hear it.

However our Lord has left this world in his ascension, with his disciples standing before him as a listening community. "A cloud received him out of their sight" (Acts 1:9). While they testify through their fixed upward gaze how much they are conscious of their dependence on him, and how much they want to be and remain his obedient hearers, they are directed by God's angel back into the world, so that they may now in their turn make men hearers of God's word. But they themselves must also remain hearers in their work. Through their whole life and work they remained faithful to this word they proclaim. And because of their work of preaching the word they had themselves to hear the word. In their longing for the return of their Master —"This Jesus, who was taken up from you into heaven, will come in the same way as you saw him go into heaven" (Acts 1:11)—they continually hear resounding within themselves the word he had brought them through his coming and which he had made explicit through his teaching and exhortation. Since then the church has never ceased to be at once hearer and preacher. Often enough the world has put the church in danger of forgetting to hear the word. But the church has never stopped listening. Against this danger God again and again raises up charismatic, prophetic men who themselves in a special degree achieve this listening which is the duty of the church. And they become a warning to all to turn back to it.

This looking and listening to the exalted Lord does not distinguish those who bear office from the lay members of the church's fellowship. All must listen. Naturally the church's disposition in office and community remains. But the hierarchical structure of the church does not have its basis in this attitude of listening to what comes down from above. In this respect the entire church is gathered as the listening community of the Lord with the receptiveness of a bride. In this listening to the exalted Lord it is not so much the bearers of office in the church but far more the charismatics and saints who are the driving power which God awakes in his church when sleep threatens to overcome the watchful listening of his word. It is especially the saints, mystics and charismatics who in their listening stand under the sway of God's irruption from on high, and they prevent the church from losing itself in worldly realms and worldly company. No matter how irrevocably the church exists in the horizontal dimension as a social force for men in this world it must never forfeit its attitude of listening for the Lord of the world to come. This is of course the reason why the church is constituted in the horizontal interrelationship of official ministry and community, for the inner structure of the church is intended to serve as a sign which again and again recalls the vertical interrelationship between the hearers in this world and him who speaks from on high.

If it is true that the church lives from the event of the word, which is not merely wrested from an historical past by human memory but which occurs wherever the church is alive, and if it is also true that the church as a sacramental and symbolic reality expresses its invisible, interior life through its visible form, then we can see why Christ has given his church a certain polarity, a form which portrays the mutual relationship of a dialog. The polarity of the church's life has its deepest extension of course in the mutual relationship of the church on earth with its glorified bridegroom. But this relationship extends into the invisible realm, and the church's bridegroom is beyond the grasp and apprehension of his bride in this world. "Do not hold me, for I have not yet ascended to the Father" (Jn 20:17), said the risen Lord when Mary Magdalene in her human affection wanted to have him with her. Now if our Lord remained thus beyond all human experience without continuing his visible earthly existence in any way, then man's endowment with grace would really be possible only as a result of our

Lord's unilateral act; it could not occur through the encounter with the Lord of grace of a man opening himself to, and freely deciding for, this Lord. God does not want his work of grace to be his own unilateral act however; rather he wishes through his word to summon man to decision. The grace of God is intended to become effective in what we might call a dialog which begins with God's challenging word and which is continued in man's answer. Our life in the power of God's word would lose its strength and reality if this word were not audible through preaching. For only in this way does it achieve that kind of reality which corresponds to man's bodily existence. Thus Christ has instituted a certain polarity in the church, because at the point where it is intended to live in the strength of the word the church needs the interrelationship of speaker and hearer, of him who communicates and him who answers.

Therefore before Christ, the word, became "silent" by ascending to his exalted life which is inaccessible to us, he made certain that his church would have something in which he would continue to be visible and audible. He confronted the listening community with the official preaching ministry. This official ministry in its service of the word represents the incarnate word of God before the community's life of faith, and presents him in its preaching. The very existence of this ministry, but even more so the exercise of its preaching task, is intended to remind the community continually that man "does not live by bread alone, but by every word that proceeds from the mouth of God" (Mt 4:4). The church's official ministry of preaching is intended to help the community be a hearer of God's word. The vertical orientation of the church listening for the Lord's word from on high is transferred by Christ's institution to the horizontal dimension of the church as a social organism. This did not happen in order to replace one of these elements with the other, but rather that the invisible partner to this dialog might achieve bodily form. The interrelation of official ministry and community on the social level is a sign and a symbolic portrayal. It points therefore beyond itself into its hidden depths. The "listening church" receives the self-communication of the glorified word by listening to the word proclaimed by the "teaching church." The community hears the Lord by listening to the church's preaching. It confesses its readiness in faith before the Lord by having the ministry of the word performed in its midst and by trying to find the depths of God's word in the word of its official ministry.

Those who are called and ordained to this official service of the word do not cease to be themselves still members of the hearing church as well. They do not lose through their ordination and assignment to the official ministry of word and sacrament the potentiality and task given to them in their baptism and confirmation.

Thus the church is fashioned in this interrelationship of preaching ministry and listening community so that God's word and man's answer may have the sphere they need in order to resound with redemptive power. This is not to deny that God's word can also resound and be effectual in the interrelationship of each member of the church with all other members, and of the church with the word. The individual also has a service of God's word to perform before the others. For our Lord wills to be present wherever two or three are gathered together in his name (Mt 18:20), and this means wherever two or three cause his word to resound in dialog with one another. But this word of God which proceeds from man to man is assured of its redemptive significance on the basis of, and within the area of, the redemptive fellowship which has been fashioned in the form of the preaching and listening church. And a further prerequisite for the redemptive significance of this individual exchange of God's word is that it participate in the dialog of word and answer carried on between the word's appointed representatives in the church's ministry and the church's community which has been raised to the status of the people of God.

The Ministry of the Word and Sacraments

What we have said of the church's ministry of the word can perhaps arouse the fear that the significance of the sacramental cult as a function of the church's life is being pushed into the background. There is in fact a danger of dissolving the dual unity of the tasks entrusted to the church's ministry by playing off one against the other. The Reformation confessions continue to present themselves in large part as the church of the word in opposition to the Catholic church as the church of the sacraments. Slogans are never really quite suitable for making reality properly recognizable. For this it is necessary to free ourselves from the either-or of the slogans and to be ready to fit the individual elements back again into the living whole from which aggressive controversy has torn them loose perhaps more than was entirely appropriate. When we admit that the theological interpretation of the preaching of God's word still has much to work out that has already been much more thoroughly worked over in the area of sacramental theology, we do so precisely because we can never admit that the Catholic understanding of the church could be characterized with the phrase "church of the sacraments," if this were intended to express the abandonment of the ministry of the word as an essential element of the church. In reality Catholic Christianity has never denied that it begins in the hearing of the word, and that the sacramental cult is the proper manner of hearing God's word, since it is the realization of this hearing in terms of a fitting answer. The Council of Trent has called baptism the sacrament of faith. Thus the hearing of the word—for that is what faith is—enters into the description of the sacrament. According to the mind of the church the sacrament can therefore never be opposed to the word, precisely because the sacrament is the seal set upon the hearing of the word.

At the same time Protestant theology has been defending itself against "placing word and sacrament in opposition to one another and even designating the division between the confessions in terms of these two concepts." The reason alleged is that "the confrontation, indeed the opposition of word and sacrament, cannot be achieved at all with the terms of the New Testament."[64] "This heightened opposition —the Protestant church is the church of the word, the Catholic church is the church of the sacraments—is simply false and must be passionately rejected, at least by Lutheran theology."[65] Such a division of two forms of the church's redemptive work between the two Christian confessions is rejected because the neglect of the sacraments is considered inconsistent with the Reformation; therefore a recovery of the sacraments is seen as a duty of Protestant theology. On the Catholic side such a division can never be recognized because it would be un-Christian to assign to the word and its proclamation a subordinate place in the area of the church's redemptive work.[66]

But this emphasis of the church's ministry of the word must not be understood to mean that the ministry of the sacraments should for this reason be pushed into the background. On the contrary it is possible for us to speak so emphatically about living from the word and about the ministry of the word's proclamation because this also says something about the sacramental cult, the administration of the sacraments. The ministry of the word would certainly not continue to be what the church necessarily understands by this expression if it did not contain the ministry of the sacraments as well. We do not mean thereby simply that what we have said about living from God's word was not intended exclusively; that is to say, we do not deny that there are in addition other tasks which must determine the church's life and ministry.

But we *do* mean more thereby. We believe that we can be so emphatic in saying that the church in its life and work lives from the word because when we say this we are always saying at the same time that the church lives from the sacraments and that it must exercise a ministry of the sacramental cult. But what does it mean to say that this statement about the word also contains a statement about the sacrament? It would be contrary to the Catholic understanding of the faith to interpret the sacrament as another kind of sermon which occurs not in the spoken word but in an applied symbol. According to such an interpretation the sacrament would, like the word, descend to us men from high, though its manner of presentation would be different. Now it certainly cannot be denied that in fact proclamation does occur also in the administration of the sacraments. But we still believe ourselves bound to maintain that the primary and immediate point of administering the sacraments is not to proclaim the word of God, even though this mission is not totally lacking in the sacraments. Karl Rahner places the proclamation of the word on the same level with the administration of the sacraments when he says: "The church in its activity makes the redemptive act of God's word present. This effectual word of God finds the supreme fulfillment of its being when the church is at work most intensely, (that is, when the church actually is in the fullest sense that which it is intended to be). And in the decisive redemptive situations of man's life this supreme fulfillment of the word takes place in the sacrament and there alone."[67] But such an assertion is of course certainly not intended to overlook the fact that word and sacrament are still specifically different from one another and that their fulfillment is not in every respect on the same level.

The preaching of the word and the administration of the sacraments are indeed of the same essence, since both are functions of the church's life. But within this category of meaning we should not simply present them as acts identical in essence. They are a living unity, one which finds its realization as a twofold unity. Because they are united as two partners in a dialog, they belong so closely together that it is impossible to speak of one without having the other in mind as well. As they actually exist in the church we do not find one without the other. The church's preaching of God's word is intended to be witnessed to and answered by listening believers through their reception of the sacraments. And the reception of the sacraments is determined by the preaching of God's word to such a degree that it can be meaningful only if it takes place in response to that preaching.

The explanation of the distinction between the preaching of God's word and the administration of the sacraments, as well as the explanation of their relationship to one another, has not infrequently been made too easy by two groups of conceptual distinctions. Both groups prove on closer inspection to be inadequate and inapt, despite the fact that they also contain much that is pertinent.

Thus the relationship between the preaching of the word and the administration of the sacraments is conceived in terms of the distinction between word and work. Preaching, according to this view, speaks of God's works and thereby makes his activity known to man. And because communication of this kind is always at the same time a promise to which man is intended to open himself, preaching is both an exhortation and a summons. God's work of grace on the other hand is ascribed exclusively to the sacraments, in distinction to the preaching of the word. And the sacraments communicate God's grace to men in instrumental efficacy. Thus the sacraments prove to be God's work, whereas preaching is merely the word which informs and promises.

Upon closer examination however this distinction proves to be totally inadequate. If the sacrament were so decidedly a work, in distinction to preaching, then it would necessarily be quite remarkable that the sacraments have as a determining principle of their form, of all things—a word.[68] Conversely it is not possible to delimit the proclamation of God's word so simply as a word in distinction to work. We have already sketched above the nearness and kinship of word and work. And we shall later be able to show to what a large degree the preaching of the word shares in the efficacy of the work.

But the second way of explaining the distinction between the preaching of the word and administration of the sacraments, namely through analogy with the mutual relationship between word and sign, is also inadequate and insufficiently clear. Certainly the word we speak is something other than the sign we give. However the difference is not so great as to make it impossible to understand the sign as a word and, conversely, the word as a sign. But it is not legitimate to describe these two functions of the church's life in terms of the twin concepts of word and sign primarily because preaching the word and administration of the sacraments are in fact mutually linked to one another. In the preaching of God's word the symbolic gestures of the preacher are joined with the orally spoken word; and the preacher frequently uses images and symbols as well to enliven his sermon. Conversely the symbolic sign of the sacrament also contains the spoken word, and as its crucial component at that. It is therefore impossible to distinguish the preaching of God's word and the administration of the sacraments by the use of the twin concepts of word and sign.

The most characteristic difference between the proclamation of God's word and the cult of the sacraments is probably to be found in the symbolic quality of both ministries. It is in what they both portray symbolically that we shall discover the distinction between preaching and the sacraments. We do not mean here however (what could also be examined but which at this point must be passed over) the content of preaching and that which is portrayed in the sacramental symbol. In both cases the content is quite comprehensive: preaching, in the last analysis, treats of God's total redemptive work in Jesus Christ; the sacraments portray the graces they impart[69]—and this is of course a very comprehensive reality, namely God himself insofar as he communicates himself to men in the image of what has taken place in Christ, in order that he may sanctify them and give them a share of his own nature. We must note however that preaching and sacrament portray a redemptive reality not only through their content but also through their actual performance. It is not only what they say but also the fact that they are performed that is a sign of a redemptive event.

For what is it that the actual preaching of God's word on the one hand and the administration of the sacraments on the other portray? When the church proclaims the word of God this event can of course be recognized quite clearly as the portrayal and imitation of that proclamation of his word which the Father himself performed as he gave his word the form of the incarnation of his only-begotten eternal son. The fathers were fond of seeing a parallel between the embodiment of the word in written form and the embodiment of the Word of God in the form of flesh in the incarnation. "As in 'the last days' the word of God came forth clothed with flesh from Mary into this world . . . so the prophets and Moses did not fail to clothe God's words in fitting garments when they brought it forth. For as he was clothed in the first case with the veil of the flesh, so he was in this second case clothed in the veil of the letter. And thus it is indeed the letter which is contemplated, as in the first case the flesh. But it is the spiritual meaning hidden within which we see, as in the first case we see the divinity."[70] Since scripture is the heart of the church's preaching this parallel may also be used to interpret preaching. The sacraments on the other hand, not so much through the content they express symbolically as through the fact of their performance, directly present Christ's death on the cross. And this is the sacrificial answer to Christ's coming which, as we have just seen, has the character of a word. This is true above all of the eucharist, which is of course the portrayal par excellence of the sacrifice of the cross within the realm of the church. But the same is true, though in a different respect in each case, of the other sacraments as well. We shall have to speak of these more explicitly in a moment.

The preaching of God's word and the administration of the sacraments are therefore related in a dialogic way. They are the word of God as effected by Christ and man's answer —also as effected by Christ. This interlocutory relationship of sermon and sacrament has been interpreted by the church as a portrayal of the interlocutory twin events of the incarnation and the sacrificial death of Christ. For the church performs its central service, the celebration of the eucharist, in twofold form in the service of the Word and the sacrifice. The service of the Word is an effectual memorial (commemoration) of the Word which comes from the Father in the incarnation, while the eucharistic sacrifice is the memorial of Christ's death on the cross.

The differing significance of these two ministries is also clear from the fact that the authority for their exercise is different. The preaching ministry takes place on the basis of the sending which is the foundation of the teaching and pastoral office, while the ministry of the sacramental cult is exercised as the result of the ordination which is the foundation of the priestly office. The church's mission continues that mission which made the son to be God's word to men in the incarnation. Ordination on the other hand imparts a share in that divine humanity which gave to Christ's humanity, through the hypostatic union with the son of God, its ordination to the ministry of priestly obedience in his whole life, an obedience that culminated in the sacrifice of the cross.[71]

The view that the preaching of God's word, which is received by listening in faith, and the celebration of the sacraments, which the recipient also celebrates by his reception of them, are related to one another like the two phases of a dialog finds a certain parallel in the structure of the discourse reported in the sixth chapter of John's gospel, where our Lord made his promise of the eucharist (26–71). There two ways of eating Christ are spoken of. These corresponded exactly to the two redemptive events through which man in the church allows what has happened in Christ to be effected in him. This he does by receiving our Lord in faith as he comes from the Father, and on the other hand by entering into and sharing in Christ's sacrifice through eating the eucharistic food. The larger first part of this discourse (up to verse 51a) speaks of the food which the Father gives: his Son, who must be eaten in faith. But we also hear of the food Christ himself gives: his flesh, given for the life of the world, a verse which may be a repetition in another form of Luke's version: ". . . my body which is given for you" (Lk 22:19).[72] In eating this food we enter therefore into the sacrifice Christ offers in order to obtain life for the world. What we do in faith when we receive the incarnate word which comes from the Father and what we do when we share in Christ's sacrifice by eating the sacramental food are related to one another like two phases of a dialog. These two actions are hearing the word and participating in the answer.

Experience has shown that people are often startled by this interpretation of the symbolic action of the sacrament and of its reception as an action whose significance points in an ascending direction, like that of a sacrifice. Let us therefore look into this matter a bit more closely. First of all preaching and the sacraments have different subjects who are portrayed in the form of the church's office holders. Preaching has its origin in the Father, as its subject. He communicates himself by having his son become man and by having the mystery of the incarnation unfolded and made explicit in the word of Christ and of the church. The sacraments on the other hand are performed and administered by Christ, the God-man. It is in his name that the officiating priest says in the celebration of the eucharist: "This is *my* body," "this is *my* blood"—things he cannot say in his own capacity, but equally impossible for him to say on behalf of the Father. "Though many ministers baptize, righteous and unrighteous, the holiness of baptism is traced back to none other than to him upon whom the dove descended and of whom it is said: 'This is he who baptizes in the Holy Spirit.' If Peter baptizes, this is he who baptizes; if Paul baptizes, this it is who baptizes; if Judas baptizes, this it is who baptizes."[73] According to the most ancient conviction of the church's tradition the actual minister of the sacraments is not the visible man; neither is it, directly, God. The actual minister is he whose sacrifice has redeemed us, the divine-human priest, Jesus Christ. This is then the fulfillment of something already recognizable in the discourse at Capernaum: the subject through whom the word which is eaten in faith is preached is different from the subject through whom the sacrament is celebrated and administered. This difference is founded, in the last analysis, in the fact that preaching descends to us from God, whereas the sacrament, like the sacrifice it represents, although it does indeed also come to us "from above"—since it is Christ who makes his sacrifice available to us for us to participate in—nevertheless ascends from us with whom the God-man dwells to the Father.

It should be emphasized however that this distribution of the acting subjects and of the direction in which the significance of their actions points, as between the preaching of the word and the administration of the sacraments, is not so exclusive that it could not also be considered differently in light of other aspects. Thus for example the sacrament, precisely because it is a "portrayal," is also a witness as well and, as such, a proclamation which shines forth in the community and in the world outside, and which thus shares in the preaching of the word. Conversely the preaching of the word, because it takes place in obedience to the divine mission communicated by the church, is the performance of a ministry which is directed upward, and participates therefore in the "ascending" direction of the sacrifice and the sacrament. Moreover the figurative conception of the word's "descent" must not be so misunderstood that it excludes the other figurative understanding of the "radiation" of the preaching in the more horizontal dimension of the community.[74] Despite all these remarks however what we have said here may well remain true: the immediate and direct significance of these two functions of the church's life engenders between them the relationship of a dialog.

It is possible to discern from the few New Testament references to the essence and nature of the sacraments that they all—and not merely the sacrament of the altar—portray the sacrifice of Christ, though under varying aspects. The evidence is most explicit with regard to that sacrament of which we can say with complete certainty that its first and immediate purpose is to represent the sacrifice of Christ on the cross,[75] namely the eucharist. Those who participate in the celebration of the eucharist are intended, while eating the body which is given and drinking the blood poured out for the sins of men, to enter into the sacrificial act that accompanies Christ, who is present "in the condition of a victim."[76]

We also find baptism referred to Christ's sacrificial death (Rom 6:3–11). It is true that it is no longer undisputed today whether the term "*homoioma*" means the sacramental act of baptism as a figurative portrayal of Christ's death and burial, or whether it signifies merely the "form" and "manner" in which Christ died.[77] But this controversy does not affect the fact that Christ's death is portrayed in the act of baptism, so that when someone enters into this sacramental act he enters into Christ's death and burial, and therefore dies and is buried with Christ.

As the third piece of evidence that a sacrament is a portrayal of Christ's sacrificial death we can cite the statements of the Epistle to the Ephesians with regard to Christian marriage (5:25–7). True, it is difficult to show the sacramentality of marriage on the basis of the text alone. But this sacramentality is established in the doctrinal teaching of the church. Therefore what the biblical text says about the meaning and substance of the marriage fellowship, about the symbolic connection between marriage and Christ's sacrificial death, does in fact apply to the sacrament of marriage. Marriage is the sacramental image and sign of that loving devotion in which Christ redeemed his bride on the cross.

Finally we can add the johannine narrative of the institution of the sacrament of penance after the resurrection (Jn 20:22f). The reference to the Holy Spirit could make us at first suspect that this sacrament's sign points not to the sacrificial death but to the sending of the Spirit on the day of Pentecost. But we must not forget that the Pentecostal breathing in of Christ's Spirit as the church's vital principle became possible only through the death on the cross. The dogmatic teaching of the church also traces the church's origin together with the Pentecostal event back to Christ's sacrificial death,[78] when the church as the new Eve came forth from the side of the second Adam after his decease. And the bible's statement also refers back in this way over the sacrament of penance to Christ's death on the cross. The cross is the seat of judgment where sin is blotted out in penance; hence it is also the pattern and source of the sacramental forgiveness of sins which takes place in ecclesiastical penance.

Finally the New Testament shows that because of the additional fact that the actual soul of the sacraments is a work they do not fall into the same category with God's word. For wherever in the New Testament a word occurs in connection with the administration of a sacrament it appears not actually as the word of God which is proclaimed, but as the praying word of the church or of Christ in the midst of his church. This confirms the upward, ascending direction of the sacramental act. The sacramental word of the eucharist, because it transforms bread and wine into Christ's flesh and blood, which in turn signify his sacrificial death, is directed like the sacrifice itself to the Father on high. The word used in the anointing of the sick ascends as the "prayer of faith" on high (Jas 5:14f). The word of ordination accompanies the laying on of hands with prayer (Acts 6:6). The word of baptism invokes the name of the triune God (Mt 28:19). The sacramental word may therefore be, indirectly, a word of proclamation as well. But directly it is "*euché,*" the imploring word of the church which is sanctified in Christ. And this word ascends, in connection with the sacrifice portrayed in the sacrament, to the Father on high. On account of the sacrifice of Christ the church is of course certain of the effect of this act which Christ has instituted. In order to express this certainty the church has in the course of time changed the verbal form of a number of the sacraments from the supplicatory to the indicative form. But just as we may not infer from the supplicatory form of a sacramental formula that the sacrament does not work "*ex opere operato,*" so the categorical statement of the sacrament's effect does not deny the fact that it is directed upward toward the Father.

Moreover the grace effected by the sacraments as well as the way they effect this grace does not in any way contradict their orientation upward toward God, but rather confirms it. In order to see this however we must consider the sacraments' causal efficacy together with their figurative symbolism. For at first the fact that the sacraments effect grace seems to indicate that their significance is to be found in the direction opposite the one we have set forth here. The sacraments are thought of as vessels or effectual causes of divine grace; and with this conception is linked at once the idea of grace as a gift coming down from on high. Now because the presentation of the vessel must have the same orientation as the content presented with it, because, that is, the causative act must proceed in the same direction as the effect it causes, the sacrament really does seem to have the same orientation in what it effects and signifies as the word of preaching: from above to us below. But this argument is deceptive.

We must pose the question: whence the sacraments obtain their power to mediate divine grace? They have this power through their intimate relationship to Christ's sacrificial death, which is the actual source of all grace. Because this sacrificial death of our Lord is portrayed in the performance of the sacraments, and because man is drawn into this sacrifice through receiving the sacraments, he gains a share in the fruit of this sacrifice, which is the grace of the Father. It is just as correct to say, on the one hand, that grace is effected through Christ's sacrifice, insofar as it is made present in the church in the outward veil of the sacrament, as to say on the other hand that grace is effected through the sacrament insofar as it is an effectual portrayal of Christ's sacrifice. The believer comes into contact with Christ's redeeming sacrifice under the veil of the sacramental action.[79] And it is through this contact that he receives a share of the grace which springs from Christ's sacrifice. But this shows clearly that the orientation attached to the performance of the sacrament does not have to be the same as that of the mediation of grace which is the sacrament's effect. Grace may come from above. But the act because of which it comes from above ascends from below, from man and the God-man to God, the giver of grace on high. The sacrifice is a human act. It is performed validly however only by the God-man, who as head of the human race ascends from among us to the Father. The sacraments are a cult in the strict and proper sense in that they portray this sacrifice.

But not even the grace effected through the sacramental act must necessarily be seen as a gift which comes down from above. If we see the giving of grace as the establishment of a divine gift in us, then this is but one of the several possible conceptions which should supplement one another. We should see grace and the sacrifice of the cross more closely and more essentially linked with one another. Man does not merely receive a gift of God objectively separate from the cross because Christ once upon a time offered his sacrifice. Grace can also and better be conceived of as the fulfillment of our participation and sharing in the sacraments. Our Lord's sacrifice is certainly not merely dying; rather it is a passage through death to the resurrection and ascension. It is the tranfiguration granted by the Father to Christ's humanity after it has been sacrificed in death. To share in his sacrifice means therefore to share not merely in his death, but also in his resurrection and ascension. Man receives in grace a share in Christ's human and divine glory. He who offers his sacrifice with Christ ascends with him in glory. This view of grace confirms, then, once again the ascending direction of the sacramental process which signifies and effects grace. When the believer receives the sacrament he allows Christ to take hold of him and carry him in his sacrifice on high into that glory full of grace (though for the time being still veiled) which is the culmination of Christ's sacrifice.

Nor does our interpretation contradict what Paul says about the celebration of the eucharist: "As often as you eat this bread and drink the cup, you proclaim the Lord's death until he comes" (1 Cor 11:26). To interpret the eucharist on the basis of this text as another kind of sermon about Christ's sacrifice would clearly contradict the eucharistic faith of the church. "In the mass a true and actual sacrifice is offered to God,"[80] "in which that bloody sacrifice offered once upon the cross is represented."[81] If the celebration of the eucharist is proclamation, then this must be understood in such a way that it does not impinge upon the sacrificial character of the eucharist and its orientation as something ascending from the God-man here below to God the Father above. There are two ways of proclaiming and bearing witness to an event. We can speak about it. But we can also join in carrying it out and thus bear witness to it before others. The first of these two ways is exemplified by the church's preaching of God's word, in which mention is of course also made of the death of our Lord. It is in the sacramental celebration, on the other hand, that we proclaim our Lord's death by joining in it. The sacrifice, sacramentally and visibly offered, is thus proclaimed at the same time to those who are able to interpret the event.

It is in just this way perhaps that the ministry of the word and the ministry of the sacraments are related to one another like the two phases of a dialog. This is the way in which the interloculatory saving event of Christ's work, also God's entrance into the world, showing himself to men through the incarnation and the preaching of the word, and finally man's answering approach to the Father in obedient sacrifice are intended to be portrayed in the church and to become effective. This dialogic relationship of proclamation of the word and administration of the sacraments will prove to be very important when we come to the question of the efficacy of the ministry of the word and its redeeming power.

PART TWO

THE EFFICACY OF GOD'S WORD

The word "actuality"—and we have been speaking above of the actuality or reality of God's word—sounds as though we could suspect that it expressed and denoted more than the mere fact that something exists. Actuality seems to denote that a thing is not only thought of or possible, but that it has been transferred from the realm of potentiality or thought into the state of actual being. However the word "actuality" (*Wirklichkeit*) really expresses more than this. It makes us suspect that a certain activity is connected with the existence of the thing, and that actuality therefore means activity too. And in point of fact the more active a being is the more actuality it possesses. And when something actual conveys actuality to another thing through its activity it must itself possess the highest degree of actuality.

Therefore when we have established the actuality of God's word we are led at once to the further question whether this word of God is also active in his church, and what kind of activity it possesses. Protestant Christianity not infrequently charges Catholic theology with having emphasized so strongly the sacraments as the instruments of God's activity in grace that there is no more room for the activity of the word. "If the Catholic church takes the sacrament seriously must it not emphasize the sacramental character of the word more strongly than it does? How could the Catholic church otherwise really provoke from its side a misunderstanding of the Lutheran doctrine of justification by speaking as though the word and judgment of God which justified us were a mere 'word,' opposite which one must place a divine act for our regeneration?"[82] At the same time however Protestant theology has quite generally admitted that even within its own ranks the word of God has not been maintained in that strict sense which is its due according to the most genuine concern of the Reformation. It is recognized how much the word of God has devolved into an intellectualized conception, so that it is completely devoid of that genuinely sacramental character as something effecting grace which was ascribed to it by the Reformation. "The verbal character of Protestant theology of which we are so proud today is nothing more than a thin spiritualism, a western evaporation of what the Old and New Testaments mean when they speak of the *dynamis* of God as the essential feature of his words."[83] In the area of Catholic theology we are beginning gradually to work out the role which is proper to the preaching of God's word in man's sanctification before God.

In what follows the fact must first be established that God's word in all the ways it is issued plays an active role in the salvation of man. We shall then show this activity to be first of all the "intentional" kind of activity which every word possesses through its communication of truth and warning. But we shall then bring out the further fact that this activity of God's word comes about because his word effectually and objectively contains God's communication of himself in grace. And finally, we shall have to place this activity of the word in its proper relationship to the activity of the sacraments.

1 The Word Is Living and Active

Western thought has long since lost the realtistic understanding of what occurs in the word. With the advancing domination of reason, knowledge has been opposed to actuality, and the word to the speaker's being. A communication of something seems to serve only the matter to be known, so that we may master it. That the speaker in speaking of something communicates and conveys himself is a notion which has largely vanished from modern man's consciousness. The word is understood merely as a means for transmitting knowledge. What a man knows is no longer a part of the person who has communicated it. It is an impersonal property that anyone could have obtained. And the person who communicates knowledge is considered to be wholly subordinate to what he communicates. The word and its actual meaning have fallen prey to an intellectualization, and the word's content has become the victim of a depersonalization. This has closed men's eyes to the most profound form of the word's actualization, and to its real significance. Now since in God's word the word is in fact found in its most actual form it cannot be surprising that people are astonished by the question whether in the case of God's word actuality and activity do not coincide, so that communication of the word is actually communication of the speaker himself. It is true that there are voices, and perhaps they are increasing, which are trying to uncover the word's character as genuine communication between two "subjects." But in the sway of that attitude which sees no further actualization of knowledge and of science than their use by man to dominate his world,[84] and under the tyranny of an even greater depersonalization, these remain voices crying in the wilderness. They are not really taken seriously. Thus it is also difficult for God's word to be understood as it is meant in revelation, namely as God himself, communicating and giving himself to man—and insofar as he does this.

When the word is intellectualized it comes to be understood merely as a vessel for communicating information about the world's reality. This is definitely not the communication of a reality itself, but merely information about such a reality. This is intended then to clear the path through which the reality itself as something quite different can be approached and assimilated. However a reality which is in itself objective and exterior to the speaker is, once it has been put into words by him, no longer "objective" and exterior, but belongs to the speaker's own inner realm. In speaking the speaker always communicates something of himself as well.

In a number of areas of human life and endeavor it is certainly justified and good to strive for objectivity. But there are limits. And men must come to see once again how greatly human life is endangered when they attempt to blot out of what is said to them the speaker's personal "you," merely in order to grasp the thing he speaks about. Then life ceases to be human. Man cannot live by the thing alone any more than he can live by bread alone. He needs the word of his fellow man, and above all the word of God—words in which the speakers communicate themselves.

This is, then, the intolerable consequence of the intellectualizing of our understanding of the word. It brings with it an anti-personal objectification of that which should be known. If the speaker is intended to enrich with his word merely the intellectual faculties of him whom he addresses, then he is in reality giving the latter something which for any length of time and in itself cannot possibly be of much great worth. In such a case he who communicates looks for something which is, in a certain sense, outside of himself. He tries to take something from the impersonal realm and convey it to the hearer's knowledge. There is therefore in the word he speaks no longer any question at all of an encounter of "I" and "thou," and of the potential human enrichment which is possible only through such an encounter. The speaker is degraded to the level of someone who merely delivers objective information that does not create an encounter in which alone men can come to be at all what they really are.

Understood in this way, the word's creative character is very much weakened. However a word is not totally without creative power even when it is understood merely as the recognizable form of an impersonal, objective reality. For in this way the objective reality still receives a new mode of being in the recognition and planning of him to whom the reality is communicated. But this is still but a weak reflection of genuine creative power. This communication of the thing hardly fashions in the hearer a new reality. In truth however such a depersonalization of our understanding of the word overlooks a factor which undeniably and in fact pertains to the word. For even when the word makes an impersonal communication the communicating person always communicates himself as well in the word. And in this way the recipient comes to share in the personal life of the other. An encounter takes place which has creative power. This encounter does not always have the same force, but the encounter *does* occur. This can and does happen perfectly only when God himself sends forth his word in grace and communicates himself to man in order to open that redemptive dialog which Christ has carried on effectually and validly, and which he offers to us to share in in his church.

We shall consider the activity of God's word first, insofar as it is the word which proceeds from the mouth of God. Then we must pose the further question whether this word of God retains its efficacy when it enters into the form of the church's preaching. But we shall be able properly to exhaust and to assess such efficacy only if we consider what it really is that, according to the testimony of revelation, God's word effects. Certain dogmatic difficulties seem to make a few limitations necessary. And these difficulties seem, at first sight, to call into question once again everything that our unencumbered look at God's own witness in revelation to the efficacy of his word was apparently capable of recognizing.

The Word from the Mouth of God

We are concerned in all our statements with the word of God as it exists in the church, that is, insofar as it reaches men here and now through the church's preaching. It has been observed that the church instituted by Christ is the only religious body—with the single exception of Buddhism—which has the sermon as an essential function of its life, as the basis of its existence now and in the future, of its encounter with the world outside the church and above all of its inner life.[85] However if the sermon is so essential and peculiar to the church, then the church's essence cannot be recognized at all if the word of God is not understood in the form it assumes in the church. The same is true if we look at the matter from the other side. God's word is effective for salvation and hence important for us men only insofar as it is present in the church and as it goes forth to us men in the church's preaching. God himself has linked the efficacy of his word with the church. Even though there seem to be hearers of God's word outside of the visible church, they no longer stand simply outside of the church; nor does God's word reach them without relation to the church. On the other hand it is difficult to be certain of the efficacy of the word precisely in the form it assumes in the church. But at the same time we have no difficulty in ascribing to the word which comes, as it were, directly from the mouth of God the character of the "two-edged sword" which the seer on Patmos saw issuing from the mouth of the Lord (Ap 1:16), a comparison also adopted by the Epistle to the Hebrews (4:12).

Now even if we are concerned above all with the word of God in the church and with its proclamation, we still cannot speak of its efficacy in this form without proceeding from God's word in the moment in which it comes forth from his mouth. For only if it proves to be efficacious there is there any point at all in proceeding to ask whether its proclamation in the church also transmits this efficacy. And yet, it can hardly be for nothing that God himself has seen to it, when he spoke in revelation, that the various forms of his communication are always denoted in a similar manner as the ministry of God's word. Of course it is analogy which links the different uses of the term "word of God" with one another. But when we see God's word portrayed in one case as an activity, then the characterization of the preaching of the church as the proclamation of God's word does not suggest at once the presumption that this proclamation transmits along with the word of God its active quality as well.

Speech within the Godhead

The faith of the church forbids us to characterize as a creative communication of the Father that speech within the Godhead in virtue of which an inner-divine word stands opposite the Father as the second person of the deity. Faith in the trinitarian God demands not only the confession of the three persons, of which the second proceeds from the first and the third from the unity of the first and second, but also the confession of the identity of the substance of the second and third persons with the substance of the Father. Karl Barth once drew attention to just how important the controversy over the smallest letter of the Greek alphabet proved to be at the Council of Nicea in the year 325.[86] If the second divine person were only *homoiusios* (of like substance) with the Father we could say, as Arius erroneously taught, that the second person was brought forth by the Father in a creative act. But if the Son is, as the council defined,[87] *homousios* (of one and the same substance) with the Father, then he cannot be brought forth in a creative act. For creation means subordination and causal dependence. Certainly it is difficult for the human mind to assume a communication within the Godhead of the one divine nature and still maintain that there cannot be in God any causal communication of being. Christian faith would rather confess that it here stands before an intense mystery that is no longer soluble than permit human reason to ascribe to God's Son a subordination to the Father—as would be the case of course between an effect and its cause. The Father possesses the single divine nature, identical in substance, uncommunicated; whereas the Son possesses this substance by receiving it from the Father. This is one of the essential statements of the mystery of the trinitarian God. And yet this giving and receiving does not signify any causal dependence of the Son, nor any priority of the Father of a natural sort, as would always be true in the case of something produced in the created realm. During a long and tedious intellectual struggle Christendom of the first centuries spelled out what can be said of the Son's origin from the Father and where the limits of this statement lie. The formation of diverse words and concepts which to the outsider may seem mere hair-splitting is in reality witness to the church's reverence for the tasks of human thought and at the same time to its reverence for the untouchable holiness of the trinitarian God. God's revelation in the Old Testament has made manifest his untouchability and transcendence in the terrible act of striking dead anyone who, even with the best intention, touched the ark of the covenant (2 S 6:6–11). And this untouchability and transcendence extends not merely to bodily touching and to the presumption of man's self-will. This untouchability of the holy God also restricts the endeavors of the human mind to those limits beyond which there can be only the darkness of mystery. Man's attempt to possess God at least by being able to explain him founders on this fact. The revealed truth that a Son stands opposite the Father, a Son of whom the Father says: "You are my Son, today have I become your Father" (Heb 1:5; Ps 2:7)—this truth also remains a mystery. And in this connection, too, various clever men of antiquity labored to use the similarity of the words to introduce a false interpretation into the relationship of the Son to the Father. And once again the correctness of theological statement depended on a single letter. For if instead of *gennetos* (begotten) the word *genetos* (became, made, from the Greek *gignesthai*) were written, then the Son would appear as a creature subordinate to the Father, as Arianism had claimed.

Precisely in his procession from the Father does the Son possess a special relationship to the creation of the world, despite the fact that these two processions are essentially different from one another. The Son, in whom the Father knows himself, is also the reflection of God's plan and idea for the world which he intends to create. The Father knows his own divine substance and places himself face to face with this substance in the Son, that he may contemplate this substance and affirm it by breathing forth the Holy Spirit in love. In the Son the Father thus also utters everything he plans in the way of existence outside of the Godhead, and which he has decided to create.

But the very fact that God's Son, his inner word, possesses the divine essence as a communication of the Father and through his procession from the Father, makes the Son the original image of the creation. The existence of the divine word as a perfect image fashioned by the Father within the Godhead has an imperfect copy in the process of creation. For this process gives the world a share, very imperfect it is true, in God's own reality, and hence causes the world to be a kind of word in which the creator gives tidings of his glory.

We do not recall this because we were concerned here with the role played by the divine word in the activity of creation outside the Godhead. Rather should the kinship which seems natural to Christian faith and which is witnessed by tradition between the process of creation and the procession of the word within the Godhead from the Father's self-knowledge remind us that God's speech within the Godhead possesses an infinite fruitfulness. What the creative power of a word means in the created realm—that power through which the word becomes active in him to whom it is spoken, that which the creative might of God's exterior proclamation of himself in the creation of the world means: all this is founded in the fact that speech between creatures and God's "speech" in the creation of the world are an imperfect copy of the speech within the Godhead and share therefore in its fruitfulness.

The word one man addresses to another is always more or less the expression and working of a love which communicates itself. And because this is so we can apply to the word the observation made by Anders Nygren about the similarity and difference of the love which obtains on the one hand among men, and between God and men on the other.[88] Even between man and man love—and therefore the word as well—is in some measure creative and spontaneous. It is true that the loving attention of the one is first set in motion by the lovableness of the other. But once it is in motion this love has a certain creative effect. The fact that one man's love comes upon another alters and enriches him who is loved. Something new arises in him. To be sure, human love can never be completely creative and spontaneous without there being an already existing lovability to bring the love of the other to life. Precisely this is the special feature in God's creative love. The love God bestows upon creatures, and upon man above all, is spontaneous and creative. God does not bestow his love because a lovable partner is there; rather man becomes lovable, indeed he first begins to exist at all, only when God bestows his love upon him.

This is so actual within the Godhead that the second person in God is at the same time the word and him to whom the word is addressed. Among men he who is spoken to is, of course, always different from the word communicated to him. Only because there is someone who can receive a word does the speaker begin to formulate his word at all. In God however he who is addressed, he to whom the Father's self-knowledge is communicated, is identical with the word. The Son comes into being by receiving the Father's word. That speech within the Godhead in which the Father utters what he knows of himself is creative and is the original pattern of all creative speech in the following sense: in this inner-divine speech the second divine person who is "addressed" does not merely receive the word; rather his divine existence is founded in this inner-divine speech.

This leads to the presumption that wherever God's word is mentioned we shall also find participation in the fruitfulness of this speech with the Godhead. We could even presume that the incarnate Son of God is called the "word" in the same passage which proclaims his preexistence within the life of the Godhead (Jn 1:1–18) precisely because these two ways in which God speaks are similar in character. Gerhard Kittel has drawn attention to the fact that in the conception of the Logos presented by the johannine prologue what is new is "not the identification of the 'word' with Jesus: this is the ever more prominent heart of all the New Testament statements on this point, so far as they are definite at all. What is new is far more that the prologue speaks of the preexistence of this Logos-Christ and that its actual theme is his transition from his preexistent state into history."[89] In his preexistent state however the word which has entered into history in the incarnation is completely creative. The second divine person possesses his being by being uttered as the word. Hence it cannot be otherwise than that this word, even when it is issued historically, is fruitful, making men to "become partakers of the divine nature" (2 Pt 1:4).

The Incarnate Word of God

Even if it is true that John in the prologue of his gospel follows God's word into his eternal preexistence, it still remains true that this eternal thought which is the Father's self-utterance within the Godhead actually becomes a "word," the instrument of divine utterance to creation, only through the incarnation. That even John means by his references to the word our Lord in his existence as the God-man can be confirmed by the first verse of his first epistle as well. There we read of the "word of life," which is, to be sure, "what was from the beginning;" but it is also "what we have heard, what we have seen with our eyes, which we have looked upon and our hands have handled" (1 Jn 1:1).

Our faith is called "Christian" not merely because the ecclesiastical fellowship of this faith was instituted by Christ and because its inner life comes from its glorified Lord. This feature alone does indeed characterize our religion decisively in comparison with all human attempts to found a religion. But the characteristic word, "Christian," goes deeper than merely to the church's origin in Christ's institution. It characterizes also the innermost substance, the redemptive meaning of our faith. This consists in the fact that we receive in faith in Jesus Christ a share in him and in his divine and human life. Believing in Christ we follow him not only as the founder of a Christian religious fellowship. Rather it is the true membership in this church which makes man Christian in his innermost being. Through the institution of his church Christ has incorporated into himself something which, as a unity of head and members, is a mystical body. In the society of this body its members are penetrated by that life which made the God-man to be the visible, humanly perceptible form and presence of God's Son. Although the members of the mystical body are not united to the Son of God hypostatically, as are the members of his physical, organic body, the connection of the living church and of its members with God's Son nevertheless remains so similar to the unity of the human Christ with God's Son, and shares to such a degree in this unity, that those who are received into Christ in grace are partakers of his divine nature. But even this is not everything which the adjective "Christian" contains as the description of the peculiar character of our religion. This mystical unity of life with Christ which our faith proclaims and imparts is distinguished from all natural and pseudo-mystical forms of religion by the fact that despite this existence in Christ the individual, personal existence of the individual is not infringed upon. The unity with God is indeed a genuine unity of life, and yet at the same time a genuine mutual relationship between partners. Man can still decide for or against God—indeed he *must* do so. In other words the living unity of redeemed man with God through the life of grace in Christ occurs through the encounter in the word. By the fact that a man has heard and answered a divine summons he has been raised in grace to life in God. Of course this is not a conversation between two partners of equal rank. Even when he addresses man in love God cannot descend to the same level with him. In a certain sense God has indeed done this in the incarnation of his Son, when he "emptied himself" (Phil 2:7) by taking on the form and substance of a slave without ceasing to be God, and by walking as man among men. But even that does not bring the partnership between him and men onto the level of equality. Our friendship with God, our status as children of the heavenly Father, our membership in Christ—none of these alters the fact that God is and remains the untouchable holy one, and that therefore man's intercourse with God must, despite all the intimacy in grace, be characterized by reverence and awe. The dialog between God and man is indeed partnership and friendship. But it is grace which gives it this quality. And no matter how deeply man may be drawn into the dialog with God, the dialog is still always opened by God and must continually be opened by him afresh. Man before God cannot of himself remain silent or speak according to his own pleasure. He can at all times only listen for God to address him, when and in the manner God chooses. And man's speech must always be an answer. It is God who here and now initiates and offers to man for his participation that dialog of revelation and faith, of grace and good works, which is grounded in the incarnate word and in his sacrifice.

When we call ourselves believers we mean of course just this: that we hear God's word in faith and thus allow the incarnation to become active in us. In the incarnation of the divine word all God's converse with men has reached its perfect climax. Everything God has spoken to men at other times is either the preparation for this definitive word or its echo and result.

The whole drama of divine redemption prior to the incarnation of the word is God's preparatory dialog with men. By creating the world through his word, as the first creation narrative testifies so impressively, God prepared the area in which the perfect communication of his word was to be issued. Thus what we may call creation's verbal character is brought to the highest supernatural perfection of its form in the incarnation of the word. And everything God says through the prophets drives his redemptive work for his people toward this climax in the incarnation of the Son. Beyond this highest of all divine words there is no further revelation of God. For how could God communicate himself any more than he has done through this "translation" of his inner word into human language and reality through the incarnation?

The incarnation of the Son in Jesus Christ is of course, in a certain sense, such a translation. Now when that process to which the word of God owes its existence in the interior life of the Trinity is transferred, as it were, into the reality of the created world which is external to God, then this speech must be creative in character. And, in fact, the sending of the Son in the incarnation corresponds in the realm exterior to God to the procession of the Son from the Father's knowledge within the interior life of the Trinity. And this sending takes place by God's creation of that human nature which is borne not by a human person but by the person of the Son of God. In this way however God's utterance proves to be productive even where the word within the Godhead receives outside of God a human form. At the point where the utterance of the divine word reaches out into the world it is creative. The sending of God's word into the world did not remain an "invisible" sending, as theology terms the sending of the Holy Spirit to bestow grace upon man. The sending of God's Son utters the same word in our history which is spoken by the Father in the interior life of God. But this sending gives the word a visible, tangible, human form. A man appears among us as God's word. The God-man is the result of a divine utterance that was at the same time a genuine creation. The word has become flesh through a genuine creation which is not merely the accompaniment of the divine utterance, but an essential part of it. The utterance in the world of the word within the Godhead does not pass away therefore like a breath of wind, but abides as the presence of God's Son in our history. And that does not even cease completely at the point where the God-man disappeared from worldly history through death, resurrection and ascension. His presence receives, rather, a certain permanence in the mystery of the church and its manifold ministry.

Now this word which came to us as the God-man in the power, fruitfulness and creative strength of the divine utterance continues its creative work. Wherever the word which is Jesus Christ comes, there it effects a "new creation" (2 Cor 5:17; Gal 6:17) provided only that it is received in faith. Again and again the church has in its devotion revered Mary's visitation of Elizabeth as the type and witness of this creative work. The child Elizabeth bore in her womb leapt when Mary brought to him the Savior, still hidden in his maternal womb (Lk 1:44). Tradition sees here a sign of

John's sanctification prior to his birth, so that the church does not hesitate to celebrate his birthday in its liturgy along with the birthdays of Mary and Christ—the only others whose birthdays are so celebrated. It is impossible to hear the word God sends men in Jesus Christ without coming to be sanctified through participation in the human and divine essence of this word. To all who receive this word power is given to become children of God (Jn 1:12).

We should also consider in this connection the miracles our Lord performed, according to the reports of the gospels. The fact that God's communication to men occurs in word and work at the same time and together has the additional consequence that these two elements of the divine activity interpret each other. The more impersonal work of God is not merely explained by his word in its meaning and purpose but is also made known as a work performed personally for us, as a gift presented by God in love. But conversely, God's work is also an interpretation of his verbal communication. This is the case precisely in those places where God's activity is intended to appear as superhuman and divine in a special way, namely in his miraculous activity. But what do the miracles our Lord performed contribute to the clarification of his word?

The matter is most frequently explained as follows: our Lord, whose words of teaching and warning come of course from God and hence demand discipleship, produced his miracles more or less as authentication of his words. God must stand behind him and his demands when he performs works of this kind which transcend all creaturely powers. The miraculous work does not occur alongside of the word he speaks, but with intentional reference to this word. The right to utter the word is proved by the miraculous work. However this relationship between God's word and his work in Christ's life is not, despite its importance, the only thing linking the two. The miracle is not merely intended to confirm that Christ's word is in truth a divine word. Rather the fact that the miracle occurs as an accompaniment of Jesus' word has interpretory significance as well. This fact is intended to demonstrate the word's power and efficacy. The miracle is the visible effect of the spoken word. "Take up your bed and walk." Our Lord commands the winds and waves. The connection between our Lord's miraculous activity and his mighty utterance manifests the effectual power of his word. This efficacy in the visible miraculous realm is, to be sure, extraordinary. This is not intended to be so at all times. But at the beginning of Christ's redemptive work an indication is to be given of the fact that even when the effect does not outwardly appear miraculous, the word of the Lord is still effectual and creative. "It is a genuinely Old Testament thought that God's word must prove to be creative in signs and wonders."[90]

The Word of Creation

We must now follow the creative character of the divine utterance further, to the third stage. This is that kind of divine utterance which stands at the beginning of all God's activity in the world, and which establishes the very existence of the reality of partnership in our confrontation with God. Before we are instructed about a word which has been uttered within God and which is "productive," before it has been revealed that this word uttered within God became man and has, therefore, been uttered to the outside, we are told: the whole world in which we listeners live, and our existence as listeners of the divine word, are themselves the result of a divine utterance. In the word of God was created the world and we in the world. The word of God displays his creative power most immediately in the created world.

In human experience, it remains certainly a secret that the word of God is the basis of the work of his creation. In the domain of the supernatural and grace-filled reality, man experiences the divine word in the form of the proclamation of the church, while the grace-filled effect of this word remains hidden to him. But the contrary is true in the domain of the reality of natural creation: man experiences his world immediately; he may also recognize that the creation has been made by God from nothing and is maintained from nothing. But the word, uttered by God when creating the world, is not accessible to man. In both cases therefore only a part of the whole is accessible to human experience: the word without its effect, or the effect without the word.

The world in which man lives, as he contemplates it, imposes upon him the duty to listen to the divine word. The existence and nature of the world prove that it results from a divine word. The world proves to be a reality of plan and reason, however difficult it may frequently be to determine individual details in this reasoned structure. Evolution too, the basic law of the world, the favorite of today's thinking, cannot accept chance, but must presuppose a plan which defines evolution and in which the seeds of all evolution must be seen as the reflection of the creative Logos. Scientific investigation of the world, and the world in wonder fulfill their purpose not when they lead to the use of this world as an inexhaustible reservoir, but when they result in the discovery of the word God has established in this world for men, in order to make known the world's meaning. "The proof of God's power is also and indeed above all God's word because the power which man encounters in nature 'says something' to him, and because man 'allows something to be said' to him through this power."[91] At the beginning of the whole world "God spoke." And this word clings to the world permanently. If man attempted to separate the world from God's utterance and consider it quite impersonally as his property, the world itself would surely take its revenge for this misuse.

But it is not only as we look back from the world as it is to its origin that we find God's word as its beginning and foundation. Conversely, too, the view of the world from God's word shows the creative character of the word of God. Where the word of God is presented to us, and even if the passage did not refer directly to the world, the word's peculiar quality is still characterized through the world the word created. The eternal and yet incarnate word of God is portrayed at the same time as also the word of creation (Jn 1:1ff). "Concerning this word of creation the following must in fact be said: *panta di autou egeneto* (all things were made through him, v 3). And he is *zoe* (life, v 4). That is simply another way of expressing the fact established in Genesis 1, namely that without the 'God spoke' no kind of creaturely life exists."[92]

Hence it can only be logically consistent to ascribe the supernatural new creation in grace to God's word. If even the natural creation of the world is ascribed to God's word, then it is all the more necessary that the newly created reality of man in grace be determined by the word of God. For grace is of course the incorporation of man into the life of the Son of God. The connection of the life of grace with God's word, and the creative character of God's word as productive of grace in the supernatural order of salvation, are suggested also by the following double consideration.

First of all we must have rightly in mind what we actually mean when we speak of grace. Certainly all that we are able to say by way of making the nature and reality of grace understandable is analogy and image. It was no coincidence that Jesus again and again expressed his preaching of grace in images. This is indeed intended to bring the reality of divine grace close to man's understanding. But at the same time it warns against the temerous opinion that human speech can exhaust the real nature of grace. The science of theology is continually in danger of breaking up into concepts what is expressed in images, and fusing with the greater clarity it has thus far to a certain degree achieved the illusion that it has comprehended the whole. This would be however a lessening of what God gives in grace—and a lessening foreign to the reality. Even conceptual work must recognize that it remains analogous, linking with the similarity of its statements things which are very dissimilar, and leaving even that which is positively stated to be, in large degree, "suspected."

Western theology has for many centuries now presented that reality we term "grace" under an aspect which is certainly correct and also very important. Through grace there arises in man a new reality, a new being. This does not, to be sure, abolish and replace man's original, natural being, nor does it superimpose something new on him. Rather it penetrates man's natural being with a new divine reality, a quality and condition or habit (*habitus*) which clings to him. However this way of looking at the matter must, if it is not to abridge the truth, take more fully into consideration the other part of that total reality which is designated by the word "grace."

For it is possible to conceive in various ways of this inner renewal of man in grace which gives him a new being. In virtue of the merit Christ won in the past through his redemptive sacrifice God creates in man here and now a new quality which establishes a new relationship to the three divine persons. Through this reality which is created in him man becomes a partaker of Christ's sonship. This means at the same time a new relationship to the Father. For Christ is of course the Father's Son. This imparts at once a new relationship to the Holy Spirit too, since he is the expression of the love between the Father and the Son. This is termed the "indwelling of the Holy Spirit." Thus grace is seen as that creative gift which is the foundation of a new relationship to the triune God, who through grace becomes the uncreated gift for man.

It is however also possible to supplement what we have said by giving to this new thing which comes about in man through God's grace another appearance. Man's sanctification can be understood as a kind of entrance of God into the personal inner realm of man. God imparts himself to man in the innermost depths of man's personality, so that he is sanctified from within and becomes something other than he was before. God becomes, so to speak, a new soul for man, a new life principle, in virtue of which man's personal decisions and actions obtain a value which immeasurably transcends all purely human significance, a value which is truly divine. Man is, as an ancient tradition put it, "made divine."[60] Grace is therefore not so much a gift God has given away and established in man to be administered by man alone, a gift which would thus experience a fate God has no control over: grace is God himself who communicates himself to man, sinks into his innermost being, and in this way sanctifies him. This sanctification makes of man a new reality not unlike the new existence effected by the soul when it animates the human body. The life of this man is now a participation in the very own life of the triune God himself. Therefore grace is related not merely to Christ's sacrifice on the cross, which is its meritorious cause, but also to the incarnation of God in Jesus Christ. For the incarnation is the exemplary cause of that which happens to man in grace: God sanctifies man by submerging himself in an individual man's history just as he consecrated the world and mankind's history in the incarnation.

At this point we must summarize what happens when God's word is uttered. What is really the intention of a word one person addresses to another? It is hard for us modern men to understand this because we have made the relationships between men much too impersonal. In our concern with the objective communication in which one man's word is intended merely to impart objective knowledge of an object, we have forgotten that a conversation is supposed to be a communication from person to person, an exchange between two subjects. The word which is the medium of conversation between men should give information about the matter at hand: that alone is crucial, according to this view. The person who informs has here no further significance except to transmit knowledge properly and, in this connection, to choose his words correctly. We are quite annoyed if the report about the object takes on subjective coloring. We are skeptical with regard to every human communication because we desire communication without any evaluation, expression of opinion or positive or negative reaction on the part of him who informs. In this age of pure objectivity and of evaluation according to the pure usefulness of things we do not want to be without a purely objective understanding of the word too.

It must of course be admitted that this objective significance also belongs to the word and to communication. But we must not overlook the fact that this is an incomplete and subordinate realization of the word's meaning. In point of fact, even in those cases where an objective communication is made in words it is never the matter in itself alone which is intended, but always the matter as the property and determining factor of him who has expressed the matter in words. When someone communicates something in a word he does not merely say: "Such and such is the case;" but rather: "I discover, feel, see it in such and such a way." In communicating the matter he always communicates at the same time something of himself as well. We are going to have to learn again that this is not a misfortune, as the impersonal thought of our objective age would like to believe. If the divine order of creation had meant our knowledge of things to be solely objective and pragmatic, God could also have made most of the things we men need for daily living directly knowable and discoverable, so that merely for our use of things we would not be quite so dependent upon encounter with our fellow men. In reality however the world of things serves men according to the divine order of creation not only through the pragmatic use of these things, but also by compelling men to speak with one another about this world of things and in so doing to communicate themselves to one another. The world of things ministers to men's personal existence by leading men to one another and by causing them to encounter each other. So that in reporting about things men are actually communicating themselves to one another.

That is the inner dynamics and tendency of the word which proceeds from one man to another. The word does indeed contain immediately a statement about things of the exterior world or about a condition in the speaker which can be objectively described. But what such a condition actually means is the speaker himself who wishes to communicate himself to the other so that he may be accepted by the other and answered with the return gift of the other's communication of himself. It is true that the word does not always come from the same inner depth. But it is never totally devoid of a connection with the speaker's innermost realm. This affects not only what is said, but also the manner in which it is said, the way the words are placed and sentences formed. "*Le style c'est l'homme*" contains a very profound truth. Hence something similar is true of verbal communication as is true of faith, for which verbal communication is the prerequisite. "The basic form of faith is not presented in the statement: 'I believe something,' in distinction to: 'I know something.'. . . The basic form of faith is expressed, rather, in the two sentences: 'I believe in you,' and 'I believe you.'. . . On the basis of this principle and basic form it is clear that faith means first of all and primarily not relationship to things, sentences and formularies, but a relationship to the person and to persons; and that faith does not move in the realm of subject and object, nor in the realm of I and it, but in the realm of the encounter between I and thou."[94] Something similar is true of the word. Even when it communicates things it is still communication of a person. And even if the personal element in the communication is not always present in the foreground in the same manner, it is never quite lacking. And the objective knowledge received through the verbal communication is always at the same time the reception of the person who communicates this knowledge—if the person who communicates does not simply use the objective content of his communication merely as a means of some sort.

Among men however this efficacy of the word very soon reaches its limit. Man cannot convey himself completely to another. The word can never do more than express to another something out of the personal inner realm and offer this for the other's acceptance. An essential communication occurs in this connection only in very limited measure. But with God the matter is different. In the utterance of the word he is able to proclaim and bring about a genuine communication of himself. He can penetrate to the innermost depths of the human person and give himself to man in grace.

These two parallel observations, that grace is God himself

who communicates himself to men, and that the word in its very nature means a communication of the speaker himself to the one whom he addresses, prepare us for what the testimony of biblical revelation clearly proclaims. There the word of God is proclaimed as something creative, as something which sanctifies and imparts grace. The New Testament speaks of the liveliness of God's word. This word grows. "The word of God increased" (Acts 6:7). "The word of God grew and multiplied" (Acts 12:24). "The word of the Lord grew and prevailed mightily" (Acts 19:20). Indeed so living is this word that it "speeds on" (2 Th 3:1). And its living quality is so mighty that it "cannot be fettered" (2 Tim 2:9). That God's word exercises a creative power is testified to by the New Testament in various statements. Christians are "born anew, not of perishable seed but of imperishable, through the living and abiding word of God" (1 Pt 1:23). "Of his own will he brought us forth by the word of truth" (Jas 1:18). So this living word of God is an event full of power. "The word of the cross is . . . the power of God" (1 Cor 1:18), "the gospel is the power of God for salvation to every one who has faith" (Rom 1:16). Such pieces of testimony leave no room for doubt that God's grace is imparted whenever God's word falls upon a man who is properly disposed to receive it. What human words aim at in vain—the speaker's bestowal of himself upon him whom he addresses—can in fact be achieved by the word of God.

All this presents no difficulty so long as it is a question of the word which proceeds from the mouth of God himself. Coming from God himself the word is always linked with his creative work. The word God speaks is a testimony and pledge of the fact that he acts on man in grace, himself penetrating man to sanctify him. "The word in the biblical sense is not only the communication of a state of affairs or of a thought, but rather revelation. More than that, it is the manifestation of a will, the ever creative will of God. In this word the creative power of God himself is at work. The word is God's creative activity in the world and especially on man (Gn 1; Ps 32:9; Sir 43:26; Hos 6:5; Ps 106:20; Jer 23:29; Is 55:10). It effects bodily healing: Mt 8:8; Lk 4:39. It casts out devils: Mk 1:25. When Jesus (in Lk 4:16–30) presents himself as the messenger of good tidings prophesied by Isaiah (31:1f) the word appears once again, referred to repeatedly by the Greek verbs *euangelizesthai* (to preach) and *keryssein* (to proclaim), as powerful to effect salvation. The disciples are clean in virtue of the word the Lord has spoken to them: Jn 15:3. Paul says that the word works among the faithful (1 Th 2:13), that it bears fruit (Col 1:5), in fact, that it is actually the power of God (1 Cor 1:18). It has the power to consecrate all things (1 Tim 4:4f; Rom 4:12; Heb 4:12f).[95]

The question of what we can say with regard to the power of God's word once it has achieved the form of the church's preaching is by no means so straightforward. We must now speak especially about this question, keeping in mind a difficulty which arises here and which we must attempt to answer at a later stage.

2 THE WORD IN THE MOUTH OF THE CHURCH

So long as we consider God's word under the aspect of the "two-edged sword" proceeding from the mouth of God (see Ap 1:16) we do not have any great difficulty in ascribing to it the sharpness testified to by the bible. Wherever the almighty, creating God speaks he links his work with his utterance in such a way that it seems like the consequence of his utterance. But the creative efficacy of God's word is not so self-evident when it is entrusted to the care of the church. The difficulty we may feel here arises not only from the fact that in the church it is, of course, human speech in which God's word is hidden: there is the additional consideration that the dogmatic statements of the church's teaching magisterium seem to tie God's work of grace so strongly to the sacraments that this work does not appear related to the other ways in which the church works. We must keep this difficulty in mind in stating, as we believe we are justified in doing here at the outset, that according to a proper interpretation of the statements of revelation God's word does not lose its redemptive power when it is brought to men through the church's preaching.

Effectual Preaching

What we have said in the foregoing about the issuance and efficacy of God's word awakes a certain nostalgia in the believer. For it points us back to a time apparently long past. In the manner in which we have hitherto considered it God's word is, of course, no longer issued. The word of God is, to be sure, not identical with revelation, but it is the organ and means of expression in which revelation is presented. Hence the suspicion may be justified that what the church states with regard to God's revelation must be true of his word as well: namely that revelation is closed with the coming of God's word in Jesus Christ, so that there is no new revelation after the close of the apostolic age. Then God's word is issued only in the dim age of the Old Testament or in the light of the New Testament, in the revelation which occurs in Jesus Christ. At any rate the issuance of God's word belongs to ages remote from our own. It thus appears that our life in the strength of God's word is not especially vital or living. It is really possible to live from a word only when the word is issued in living fashion and when it can be heard and answered just as lively.

But this fear is only partly justified. God's word does find in Jesus Christ the actual termination of its promulgation; there is subsequently no fresh promulgation of the word. But a mysterious dwelling place is established in the church for this divine word which has been promulgated in Jesus Christ in its final, valid form. And precisely because of this mysterious character this dwelling place is continually misunderstood. The church is, on the one hand, an institution and thus something established and abiding once and for all. In it God's word is, in a certain sense, laid up, established like something "left in trust" (*paratheke:* see 1 Tim 6:20; 2 Tim 1:12). That looks very static and moribund. But the word in the church is not like something dead, once and for all uttered and promulgated, with its content at most only repeatable. On the contrary, in the church the promulgation of the divine word is also mystically preserved just as the event of Christ's sacrifice is preserved in the church. This is certainly difficult to understand. Preserved means of course put away, set aside somewhere like something material, in order to be brought forth again and again. But promulgation denotes an event, an action, a dynamic reality.

But this is precisely the mystery of the church, which is built by our Lord "in order to accomplish his saving work of redemption perpetually."[96] This sentence from the church's teaching expresses the same contrast in meaning which we have noted just above. Permanency is ascribed here to something which apparently cannot possess it at all. Christ's saving work of redemption remains permanent like a thing and is still something actual like a work. It is the mystery of the church that in its vital functions which have been instituted by Christ, no new word of God is promulgated, but that the word promulgated once and for all is proclaimed and testified to; and that this is not a moribund repetition but the promulgation of one and the same divine word. "It is not a concept which stands at the beginning of the train of thought which is described by the word 'Logos,' but that actual event in which God makes himself known, in which he causes a 'word' to occur. Just how original and lively was the development of thought from this point in the apostolic age, and how little the concept contained in a word forms the commencement of this development, is especially clear from the fact that statements of this kind are not linked with the word 'Logos' at all."[97]

The men who live in the church today do not therefore need to forego the impact of the word as it goes forth. The mystical life of the church which proclaims God's word assures them that they are no less vividly touched and summoned by God's word than the men of Jesus' time and the men of the Old Testament. This word which goes forth in the church's preaching is not a new word of God. It is God's word at the climax of its promulgation in Jesus Christ.

But the converse is also true as well, namely that God's word is promulgated not merely in truth in the preaching of the church, but also exclusively through the church's preaching. The church is, in fact, instituted in an entirely special and very strict sense in the word of God and for the sake of its proclamation. The church is in its innermost essence the community of those who hear the word of God and heed it. And the mutual relationship of official ministry and community in the church is, in the first place, the realization of the mutual relationship between those who speak and those who hear. For the bearers of spiritual office are of course first of all the portrayers and representatives of our Lord who comes to men as the word of God in order to redeem them. And the word of God does not now seek to come to men in any other way than through the preaching church. "The concept of the word of God is [in the New Testament] characterized practically exclusively by the fact that it is issued to men in human speech."[98] "The word of God and the word of the apostle, the apostle's word and Christ's word, obviously coincide so closely, or exist, at any rate, so much in one another, that in hearing the one, the apostolic word, it is possible to hear the other, the word of God or of Christ. God and Christ speak in, with and under men's words. Man—in this case the apostle—speaks the word of God and of Christ."[99] Of course the word of God is also proclaimed when the faithful speak with each other. "As each has received a gift, employ it for one another, as good stewards of God's varied grace: whoever speaks, as one who utters oracles of God . . ." (1 Pt 4:10f). And again: "Where two or three are gathered in my name, there am I in the midst of them" (Mt 18:20). But that is a participation in the promulgation of God's word in the strictest and fullest sense through the "ministry of the word" (Acts 6:4) in that proclamation performed by the church's official ministry in its mystical portrayal of our Lord and of his utterance. "When the term 'God's word' denotes in its greatness that for which it is generally used it is the Christian *kerygma*."[100]

Against this view it cannot be said that God's word exists, after all, in a unique way in the written word of the bible and can therefore be taken up and read by each individual without his being dependent upon the preaching of the church. For when the individual Christian reads holy scripture in faith he is not meeting the word of God apart from the church's preaching. For it is the church which has transmitted holy scripture to him. And the church must open to him the meaning of holy scripture. The sense of scripture is realized only if and insofar as it is received and read as the church's book.

The church's preaching must be heard as it was by the Christians at Thessalonica, to whom Paul writes: "Therefore we too give thanks to God without ceasing, because when you heard and received from us the word of God, you welcomed it not as the word of men, but, as it truly is, the word of God . . ." (1 Th 2:13). But then this word of God must possess in its ecclesiastical form that reality which God's word cannot lose when it comes into the church. Paul bears witness to this when, in the same letter, he continues: ". . . the word of God, who works in you who have believed" (v 14). Previously he has said: "Our gospel was not delivered to you in word only, but in power also, and in the Holy Spirit, and in much fullness" (1 Th 1:5). If the church's preaching is God's word, and if God's word is creative and active, then the church's word of proclamation must also possess creative efficacy. What happened on the occasion of the apostle Peter's sermon is certainly unique, because it belongs to those things which are peculiar to the apostolic age: "While Peter was still speaking these words, the Holy Spirit came upon all who were listening to his message"* (Acts 10:44). But the unique feature lies really not so much in the fact that the Holy Spirit descends upon the hearers in the word of preaching, but rather that this occurs here in a perceptible manner. That may well have happened as a sign of the power which lies in the depths of the church's proclamation of God's word. In the Acts of the Apostles "the emphasis is placed upon the fact that the word [of preaching] leads to salvation (11:14; 13:26), that it is the bearer of grace (14:3; 20:32;

* ". . . fell on all them that heard the word" in Douay-Rheims version. —Ed.

see 20:24) and that it builds up the Christian fellowship and leads to eternal life (5:20; 10:36; 13:15)."[101]

This peculiar efficacy of the preaching of God's word is demonstrated also by the fact that it is not bound causally to man's decision and personal attitude. "The personal motives of the preacher are not of first importance. Already in the New Testament it is necessary to speak of humanly inadequate motives for preaching (Phil 1:15–18). Hearers can be won for the faith even by a sermon preached out of impure motives. If then the preacher's religious or ethical personality is not decisive for the efficacy of the word, precisely because the word's power does not lie in human capability but in God's might, there are all the same unqualified obligations for the preacher. . . . These are not required of him however on account of the word, as if the word were, so to speak, dependent upon his fulfillment of these obligations, but rather for the sake of the preacher himself, lest, when preaching to others, he himself should be a castaway (1 Cor 9:27)."[102] And when subdeacon and deacon receive at their ordinations the commission and authority "to read the epistle, or the gospel, in the church both for the living and for the dead,"[103] a kind of efficacy seems to be presupposed here for the proclamation of the word which does not culminate in stirring the hearers morally. For the dead cannot be morally influenced any longer. If the word of God is nevertheless to affect them, then it must in some way proceed from God objectively, actively in grace, and creatively.

According to the exegetical interpretation of those texts which attach to the word a content in the genitive case, these texts are dealing not merely with what the word speaks about, but also with what is imparted through the proclamation of the word. "When in the apostolic preaching we read of the 'word of life' (Phil 2:16), or of salvation (Acts

3:16), or the word of the grace of God (Acts 14:3; 20:32), this means not merely that the word speaks of the life, salvation or grace which have occurred; what it means far more is that the word in speaking of these things effects life, salvation and grace. And the word of truth (Eph 1:13; Col 1:5; 2 Tim 2:15) is the word which effects truth in the biblical sense, by stripping things bare, as they stand bare before God. So also the word of reconciliation (2 Cor 5:18f) is that word which brings about reconciliation between God and the world."[104]

Rivalry between Word and Sacrament?

What holy scripture says about the efficacy which God's word also possesses in the form of the church's preaching seems to explain very simply and directly the connection between the effect, which is God's grace, and its cause, which is the church's preaching of God's word. Where the New Testament portrays the missionary activity of the church, proclamation of the word and the bestowal of grace stand so much in the foreground that we could be inclined to conceive of the two as being in fact directly connected with each other. Among the functions of the church's life as depicted by the New Testament it is undeniably the ministry of the word which occupies the foreground. Everything else must give place to this, as the apostles confess when the other tasks of the church's communal life threaten to grow up over their heads. Because, in consequence of this situation, they cannot rightly exercise the ministry of the word, which is their proper and primary task, they appoint helpers for themselves. As the Acts of the Apostles continues, it then becomes clear that even these helpers stand in a special way in the service of the word. On the other hand the church of the New Testament shows itself to be the mediator of the Lord's grace to men. In this sense also the church is the bride of the exalted Lord; for the church is intended, in union with him, to impart to the individual Christian, as his mother, the life of redemptive grace. What then is more natural than the presumption that the manner in which the church is intended to impart this grace to men is precisely through its preaching of the word of God?

But there is one great difficulty. The church's dogmatic teaching makes it no longer possible to say this so simply. The teaching of the church links the bestowal of divine grace explicitly not to the preaching of God's word, but to the administration of the sacraments. Indeed, at first sight, we could even get the impression here that the church's dogmatic teaching has been brought into opposition with holy scripture. For the emphasis with which holy scripture seems to link the church's mediation of salvation with the preaching of God's word appears to be quite as great as the exclusiveness with which the church seems to link its mediation of salvation with the sacraments. The statements of both sources sound verily exclusive. The Council of Trent in its seventh session introduces the doctrine of the sacraments with the statement that "through the sacraments all true justification begins, increases or is restored after its loss."[105] In its canons concerning the doctrine of the sacraments in general the council anathematizes anyone who says: "The sacraments of the new covenant are not necessary to salvation, but superfluous, and without them, or without the desire for them, men can attain from God the grace of justification through faith alone."[106] Now inasmuch as the terms "beginning," "increase" and "restoration" denote all the phases in which the bestowal of grace, or justification, can occur, and since the actual reception of the sacraments is necessary to salvation, or at least the desire to receive them, then it does seem as though hearing the preaching of God's word is excluded as a way of salvation and a means of imparting grace alongside the sacraments. This seems to make questionable whether the bestowal of grace upon man can be ascribed to the church's preaching of the word, an ascription we thought we had found in the evidence of the New Testament.

Medieval theology displays a clear development toward a distinction between sermon and sacrament with regard to their efficacy for grace. The earlier theology with its strong exegetical orientation "very often finds images which are intended to throw light on the nature and efficacy of the sermon. The preacher is a kinsman of Christ, a herald of God, an archer, a wine-grower. But he is also God's mouthpiece, the eye of the church, the bride's neck in the Canticle of Canticles, the maternal breast of holy church. The preacher is God's horse, a cow that pulls the cart with the ark of the covenant, an ox in God's acre; he is a way to Jerusalem, salt, a spring, heaven, and so forth."[107] Scholastic theology on the other hand works out more and more the distinction between sermon and sacrament with regard to their efficacy. "St. Thomas is not of the opinion that through the sermon an inner grace is imparted to the hearer, nor even an actual grace. Here lies, according to Thomistic theory, the essential difference between sermon and sacrament. This difference is more distinct in the theology of St. Thomas than in the previous schools. The ealier theologians thought that grace was created by God. And so it was easier for them to put sermon and the sacraments on the same level as means for attaining grace."[108]

Nor is it possible to solve this difficulty by interpreting the church's preaching of the word of God as itself a sacrament. In point of fact the church's ministry of the word does, it is true, seem to contain all the elements proper to a sacrament. It cannot be doubted that in the church's ministry of preaching a visible act portrays an invisible act of God by means of signs. And the institution of the sermon by Christ links the preaching of God's word as it does the administration of the sacraments to the church's life until the end of time. Our Lord sent his church forth into history with the command to his apostles: "Go and make disciples of all nations, baptizing them . . . and teaching . . ." (Mt 28:19). Paul has testified clearly that the church's work of preaching belongs to its foundation: "God was in Christ reconciling the world to himself . . . and entrusting to us the message of reconciliation" (2 Cor 5:19).[109] Now if it also pertains to the church's work of preaching to effect grace, then we could very well get the idea of placing the sermon in the church as a sacrament alongside the seven other sacraments.

The ascription of all justifying grace to the sacraments would thus be safeguarded, it is true, without any denial of justifying grace to the sermon—which would then of course itself be a sacrament. Nevertheless this solution does not offer an answer to the difficulty. For the church has established in a definitive dogmatic decision that there are no more and no less than the seven sacraments listed specifically by the Council of Trent: baptism, confirmation, the eucharist, penance, holy orders, marriage and extreme unction.[110] Hence it is impossible to put the church's preaching of the word as an eighth sacrament alongside the other seven. Therefore if holy scripture really ascribes to the church's proclamation of the word of God not merely a teaching and exhortatory efficacy, but the bestowal of grace as well, then we must find some other explanation for this fact. It is not enough to claim that according to the statement of revelation the church's preaching effects grace. It is not even enough to say that the sermon has an efficacy of its own different from that of the sacrament. Precisely here lies the difficulty, of course. We must so define this characteristic of the sermon that it does not cease to be a genuine efficacy, but also without its approaching too closely the unique character of the sacraments. "The redemptive dynamics of the church's proclamation of the word must not be equated with the redemptive power of the sacraments. . . . We do not have any way of describing exactly how the Spirit works in the word. It is necessary simply to avoid the two extremes; of seeing, on the one hand, in the church's word an empty word, and on the other hand of understanding the redemptive efficacy of the church's proclamation of the word as a sacramental event. We would also fail to do justice to the preaching of the word if we saw in it only an emotional force like that which the human word can possess in the natural realm. . . . This potentiality, the natural motivating power of the human word, is also meant when reference is made to the spiritual dynamics of the church's preaching of the word. But something more than that must be said, for there is a heavenly power which comes from God at work in the church's word."[111]

Various attempts have been made to explain the genuine connection of the proclamation of the word with grace in such a way that the unique importance of the sacraments is not thereby called into question. A first group of such attempts does indeed ascribe a genuine efficacy to God's word, but traces this to the impression made by the sermon's content. Of course this content can become effectual only insofar as it is preached. Therefore even in this view the actual preaching cannot be ignored, and in fact is not ignored. But what preaching effects in men's minds and wills it effects through its content. What the church is able to report of God's saving work acts by instructing man's mind and by moving his will. In this way man is moved to open himself to God's work of grace. But grace itself is conveyed through another activity of the church, namely the sacrament which works interiorly in a man properly disposed internally for its reception. Since however man can dispose himself for the reception of the justifying grace of salvation only through the workings of prevenient grace,[112] it is entirely probable that the bestowal of this auxiliary grace which touches man inwardly is connected with the disposing work of the preaching of God's word.

In this way the famous Tübingen dogmatician J. E. Kuhn, as long as a hundred years ago, strongly supported the importance of the church's preaching for salvation,[113] and ascribed to word and sacrament "the same dignity."[114] "How is it that we are conducted through the word of the gospel to faith? . . . It is not from us and in our own power but through God's grace that we come to believe . . . The divine Spirit works directly upon the human spirit, assimilating it at the same time unto himself, and fashioning it into a *pneuma hagion* [holy spirit]. Only when the divine Spirit works upon the spirit of man does the word of God find in virtue of its own power a response in the spirit of man. Only then does the power of the preacher's conviction find an echo in the hearers. And in such a manner, at once natural and supernatural, is faith engendered."[115] Despite this assurance however Khun immediately proceeds to retract his assertion that the preaching of the word effects grace. "The word is not an instrument of grace in the proper sense. No grace is attached to it, neither the forgiveness of sins nor the renewal of the inner man. Rather we are conducted to faith through the preaching of the gospel, and through the hearing of the word to faith. And then as believers we are justified through the instrumentality of the sacrament."[116] There can be no doubt that this statement deserves recognition. Whether it explains fully all that pertains to the redemptive efficacy which occurs in preaching we must however investigate. For it does seem questionable that Kuhn attempts to distinguish the preaching of the word from the sacrament as follows: "Because the word of God effects faith merely *ex opere operantis,* that is, only according to the measure of the proper and respondent activity of him who hears and understands."[117] In this point it is quite certain that the distinction between preaching of the word and administration of the sacraments is not correctly drawn. For even the sacrament, which most certainly works *ex opere operato,* becomes effective only according to the measure of the proper and respondent activity of the recipient, "according to each individual's own preparation and cooperation."[118] The expression "*ex opere operantis*" does not of course say anything at all about the measure of the recipient's own action, but only denotes this action as the cause and source of grace. But this meaning has been excluded by Kuhn himself even from the engendering of faith through the sermon.

It seems to be no less fruitless to say that the preaching of the word is charged with the Spirit if the function of preaching is then limited to the announcement of grace in distinction to its bestowal—which is the opinion of Viktor Warnach.[119] This does result, on the one hand, in a creative understanding of the word. "In its deepest essence preaching is, in a certain sense, an active participation in the original creation and in the new creation at the end of time."[120] But on the other hand the efficacy of preaching is limited once more to the announcement of a preparation for salvation. "The word is accompanied by the demonstration of the Spirit's power (1 Cor 2:4), it bears itself the power of God (1:18). Yet in the word grace is only announced and offered, not yet effectually mediated and applied. The word bears witness to salvation, but does not effect it. In the word God is present as he who reveals himself. In the sacrament however he is present as he who acts."[121] One remark of Warnach however does seem important: when he interprets word and sacrament as linked in an intimate unity: "The sacrament is intended to effect what the word signifies; and the sacrament cannot effect anything else but what is testified to by the word. Since the word through its witness to grace engenders faith in the hearer it is the fundamental element in the achievement of salvation. The sacrament on the other hand is the edifying and completing element. Only in the sacrament does the faith which is testified to through the word become fully effective for the healing of man's entire being. Hence when the word awakes justifying faith it is from inner necessity a faith that leads to baptism and to the eucharist (Acts 2:37–41; 8:12, 35–38)."[122] Here we have, incidentally, quite certainly the beginning of the correct interpretation of the relationship between word and sacrament and of the efficacy of preaching for grace.

This interpretation we have just now presented, and which is, with some variations, held by various others,[123] can hardly be doubted in what it says positively. But there seem to be some points which are not yet adequately solved. Thus we should like first of all to ask whether this view does not ascribe the efficacy and symbolic significance of the church's preaching too exclusively to the content of this preaching. Is sufficient account taken of the possibility that the actual preaching of the sermon in the church may have been instituted as a sign that God's word is promulgated ever new to man? It is precisely when we confront sermon and sacrament with one another under this aspect that the view we have mentioned proves to be insufficient and inapt. For the view seems to claim that the sermon is distinguished from the sacrament by the fact that in the sermon something is expressed, whereas in the administration of the sacrament something is effected. That through the sacrament something is effected allows of no doubt. But can we agree with the apparent presupposition implied by this manner of contrasting the sacrament with the sermon? Is the sacrament not a statement and a communication? Something is expressed through signs and symbols too. And especially is this the case when the symbolic action is accompanied and determined by a word, as is the case in the sacraments. If it is impossible therefore to contrast the sacrament as a (mere) work with the sermon, considered as the word, then we are led to the following dilemma: either we admit that the sacrament's character as a work does not exclude its character as a verbal or symbolic statement—in which case however we must also reckon with the possibility that the verbal character of preaching can include an efficacy such as is proper to a genuine work. Or else we deny this possibility with respect to the word, in which case we must think up an explanation for allowing the connection of the word or sign with the work to stand in the case of the sacrament.

Another view which also seems correct in what it says without saying everything is that the word of preaching will, as the result of a divine guarantee, be preserved from error. "The independence of the priestly power from human worthiness and unworthiness is exactly parallel to the infallibility of the church's teaching magisterium. They are the two poles of the church's sacramental reality. . . . The guarantee of the Spirit who 'will teach us all things, and bring to our remembrance all that Christ has said to us' (Jn 14:26) means therefore that the word which belongs to the church as a sacramental sign will also not depart from Christ's Spirit in the continued and essentially historical existence of revelation."[124] This view also reckons only with the content of preaching and not with its actual performance. Then we would like to ask whether infallibility, understood as the preservation of the content from error, is not but one side of the guarantee God attaches to the actual preaching of the word, and whether this guarantee cannot have another and parallel side as well, namely the word's efficacy for grace.

A further view makes too little a distinction between the preaching of the word and the administration of the sacraments. Thus the Reformation, at least as it is understood by many Protestant theologians, sees in the sacrament another kind of sermon.[125] The sacrament's task, like that of the sermon, is to arouse the hearers' trusting faith, on the basis of which the believer then attains justification. The sacrament is affixed like a seal to the word of promise proclaimed in the sermon, but stands essentially on the same level as the word of the sermon. Thus the efficacy this view ascribes to the sacrament is no different from that of the sermon. This efficacy is however, according to the theology of the Reformation, a genuine efficacy for salvation.

Catholic theologians have on occasion also considered the sacrament the supreme and complete form of the proclamation of God's word. But the special element consists precisely in the fact that proclamation in the form of the sacrament, and only such proclamation, effects grace. And if efficacy for grace is a property of other forms in which God's word is proclaimed, then they possess this efficacy only to the degree in which they participate in the sacrament. What all proclamation of the word really aims at, but can realize only imperfectly, actually comes to fulfillment in the perfect form of preaching, namely in the administration of the sacrament.[126] It may be asked here whether this view does not encroach upon the proclamation of the word in its actual and proper sense. For according to this view the actual preaching of the word is a deficient mode of the presence of God's word in the church. It is not actually in the sermon that God's word is preached in the fullest sense, but in the administration of the sacrament. Thus it seems as if the unity of word and sacrament is achieved here by a devaluation of the word. But it also seems as if this view does not take sufficient account of the fact that the word of the sermon and the word (and work) of the sacrament, although both stem from him who holds office in the church, are not spoken and performed on the basis of the same authority, nor in representation of the same actual officiant. The word of preaching is the word of the Father who speaks to us in Jesus Christ. It is Christ's word only insofar as Christ is himself the original and basic form of God's word—which is however the word of the Father. The word (and work) of the sacrament is spoken and performed by the God-man who leads us in sacrifice to the Father—and to the extent that he does this. The sacrament is performed by the church, which is aware that it is met together in Christ and is placed on the way to the Father. The sacrament is therefore the most perfect expression of faith insofar as it gives to the word of God which has been received in faith the response of active participation in Christ's sacrifice in the sacrament.

If we wish now to take the efficacy of the word's proclamation as seriously as the New Testament seems to demand, and yet at the same time preserve the uniqueness of the sacraments in their efficacy for grace, then we must proceed in two steps. The proclamation of God's word is, like the original promulgation of the word of God in Christ himself, something which exists on two levels. And together these levels make up the single reality of the word as it goes forth, and they are likewise one in their efficacy. When God's word is promulgated a content is preached. In posing the question of the word's efficacy we must not separate the content from its preaching. But the efficacy stems from both elements. And it seems as if each of the two possesses in fact a characteristic efficacy. In what follows we shall look first at the efficacy of the content of the word's proclamation, and then we shall ask further whether perhaps the event of preaching as such could also be a sign of a redemptive event, and hence perhaps the source of a proper redemptive activity as well.

2 Preaching as a Communication which Summons

However the efficacy of the preaching of God's word may be interpreted it is quite impossible to ignore its content. This is true even when it is a question of the manner in which the preaching of God's word serves the imparting of salvation. We believe we shall be able to state later that the actual preaching, as an event, has a symbolic power of its own apart from its content, and hence that it has its own significance for the achievement of man's salvation as well. And yet, neither the forcefulness of expression possessed by the content which comes to the hearer in preaching, nor the efficacy of this content, may be overlooked or neglected. This simply because preaching can of course occur only with a content. There cannot be any preaching at all unless *something* is preached. But more than that, the content that is preached serves through its motivating power to challenge and to prepare the coming of a power which is efficacious of grace and which we can perhaps attribute to the act of preaching. Hence our first question must concern the significance and efficacy of the content of the church's preaching.

1 The Mediation of Salvation through Preaching

It is rightly emphasized that the question of the significance and efficacy of the preaching of the word must be so posed that the special character of the word as precisely a word is respected. "If the many-sided apostolic preaching of the gospel makes Christ and his saving benefits to be really present, there still remains the question of the mode of this presence. In what kind of presence does the heavenly *kyrios* [Lord] reveal himself through the gospel? In the mode of the word is the seemingly self-evident answer which must nevertheless be specially emphasized! For there is also the mode of the sacrament, which is different from the mode of the word . . . To the word however belongs hearing. Thus we can also say, if we consider the way we approach the word, that the *kyrios* is present in the mode of hearing."[127] The liturgical renewal of the last decades has reminded us, even with regard to the sacraments and their significance for salvation, that this statement is important. The sacraments are frequently distinguished in an oversimplified way as works from preaching, considered as a word. Hence the efficacy of preaching is interpreted solely according to the intellectual and moral manner of the word, whereas the sacraments' efficacy is judged objectively, as is the case with a work. But the correct understanding of the liturgy and the sacraments has become aware once again of the fact that this antithesis cannot be completely true, at least not in the case of the sacraments. For what characterizes the sacrament first of all is—as Aquinas says at the beginning of the doctrine of the sacraments in his *Summa*—that the sacraments are signs and symbols.[128] But if this is taken seriously then the assignment of word and work to preaching and sacrament respectively is no longer possible. For a symbolic sign like the sacrament is also a kind of word, especially in view of the fact that it is an explicit word which makes it unambiguously sacramental. In the sacrament too something is communicated. The communication of something in the sacrament is supposed to summon the recipient to a decision for what is intended to be effected in grace through the sacramental sign. Before it is effected it is expressed through the symbolic sign. "The sacraments work by signifying" has been said even by Thomas Aquinas.[129] Therefore if the content communicated in word or sign is important even in the case of the sacraments, it is all the more important in that function of the church's life which has even more than the sacraments the character of a statement and which has been instituted to communicate contents, namely the preaching of God's word.

The Word as Communication

According to what we have said then, the sacrament has a certain similarity to preaching. Something is expressed also in the sacramental sign and word. A certain portion of Christ's redemptive work is portrayed to men in the sacrament. And men express their devotion to God by participating in Christ's sacrifice through receiving the sacrament. But at the same time the difference cannot be mistaken. The preaching of God's word has the character of a communication far more than the administration of the sacraments does. This alone is shown through the far greater breadth and fullness of what can be communicated by the church's messenger in preaching God's word, as opposed to what is expressed in the administration of the sacrament through the symbolism of one of the seven sacramental signs. It is of course not for nothing that the church supplements through the unfolding of its liturgical symbolism the lack of diversity and multiformity which characterizes the sacrament's symbolic sign. And there are still seven sacramental signs with various forms. But what is this diversity in comparison to the wealth of possibilities which exists in the preaching of God's word? The preacher can present to his hearers the entire breadth of God's saving acts. And, depending on his skill, he can unfold his material before the faithful in so many different modes of presentation that the cult of the sacraments simply cannot compete.

This difference alone may show that the preaching of God's word is oriented in a special way toward that content which is the sermon's particular task to communicate.

This difference between the sacraments and the preaching of God's word is not so surprising as it may seem at first sight. It is perhaps initially extraordinary that the communication of man's devotion to God in Christ's sacrifice, which is expressed in the sacraments, has so much narrower a range of varieties for its expression than the preaching of God's word, in which God's devotion to men is expressed. Precisely when preaching and the administration of the sacraments as the portrayal of the incarnation and sacrifice present the redemptive dialog between God and men might we expect that man's possibilities of expression would be no less copious than those available to the church's preaching in which God is brought to men.

Upon closer inspection however this is not so suprising at all. In the preaching of God's word it is of course the eternal and mysterious God who comes to men, communicating himself to them and summoning them. But God possesses such an unending wealth of reality, and his redemptive work in human history is so manifold, that the content of the preaching which is supposed to speak of these things must be unending. The preacher of God's word can and must continually bring forth new material from God's revealed communication of himself; and he has also the possibility and duty of setting all this forth before men. When on the other hand man wishes to make his answer to this divine communication by participating in Christ's sacrifice, there is no need at all of so many and such diverse forms of expression. It is, to be sure, always man, in various situations in his life, but still man who must give himself to God and express himself to God. And man is not so mysterious to himself, and above all not so mysterious to God, that he must express his hidden inner depths before God in ever new verbal form. The sacramental signs and their arrangement in the liturgical celebration of the church and in personal prayer can be limited to a far smaller measure of different forms. Man can always bring himself completely into these signs no matter how different his inner and outer situation may be from what it was yesterday or will be tomorrow. There is, after all, but one single valid way to respond in self-devotion to what God has communicated. This response consists in man's participation in Christ's sacrifice by his reception of the sacrament.

The preaching of the word in which God himself makes his self-communication to men must embrace a very much richer content. The church does indeed preach in everything but one single subject: God. It speaks always about God in his word. But it is only in himself that God is a simple being without diversity and parts. He communicates himself exteriorly in an unlimited fullness of creative and redemptive acts. The activity of this one God is history: creation and the drama of redemption. But history is always diverse and differentiated. The speech through which God interprets his activity and animates it has a personal gift, for man must therefore communicate an abundance of individual acts in a variety of separate statements. Precisely because the preaching of God's word is preaching about God it contains an inexhaustible fullness of communications.

God's redemptive work is historical and social, and yet at the same time above history and individual. It is true that God performs his work of salvation for the individual men whom he wants to include in his triune, divine life. And yet his redemptive work is not intended to reach the individual directly but by means of the community whose historical and social unity are found in certain points and perfectly at Christ's entrance into history. But it is from these points that God wishes to have his redemptive activity reach all men in history. Therefore his redemptive activity is at the same time above history. Simply God's activity affects directly the fellowship of the people of God and of the church. But it is intended for the individual man, and is therefore also individual.

In its twofold character as historical and yet transcending history, as collective and yet individual, God's redemptive activity confirms that men are the image of his own eternal threefold being. God exists in three persons, but these three have a single divine nature. A faint but nevertheless genuine image of this is the existence of individual men in the unity of community and history. Hence God's activity cannot be intended solely for the community or for history without affecting the individual man, nor can it be bestowed individually upon each single man without bothering about his existence in community and history. God's redemptive work affects the individual in the form of his participation in the redemptive drama of the people of God. And what God effects in the redemptive drama of his people must be taken out of this generality and past and be worked out in the concrete present of the individual man.

This is the end which the church's preaching is intended to serve. What God has accomplished in the past for the community of his people must be brought out of this remoteness into challenging proximity with the individual man. This does not take place through repetition of the historical saving acts in the present life of the individual. Then they would no longer be acts performed for all. Rather the redemptive work of history is portrayed to, and thus brought to the knowledge of men as they live here and now, and is laid before them for their decision.

Now this occurs primarily through the church's preaching of the mighty acts of God. Though we are here concerned above all with public preaching to the individual before the people of God, still we must not overlook the fact that there is also a preaching which proceeds from the individual in whose hidden inner life God has been at work, and which is addressed to the church at large. "I announced your justice in the vast assembly; I did not restrain my lips, as you, O Lord, know. Your justice I kept not hid within my heart; your faithfulness and your salvation I have spoken of; I have made no secret of your kindness and your truth in the vast assembly" (Ps 39 [40]:10–12). In those cases where God bestows the gift of his redemptive work directly upon the individual this may not remain shut up in this individual. Indeed he may be the very one through whom God's mighty work in history seeks entry into the history and fellowship of his people.

But above all, the historical and collective church must bear witness to its members through its preaching to what God has done in the drama of redemption, and thus open this divine work to their participation. Ever since the church on the first day of Pentecost began its life which is animated by the Holy Spirit, men "hear them declaring in their own languages the wonderful works of God" (Acts 2:11). It is this preaching which first makes known to men the mighty acts through which God has made of history the drama of redemption. A reality in which man is intended to submerge himself is however in proximity to him only when he takes note of this reality and brings it into his inner consciousness. For this reason therefore that reality hidden in the historical past or in the mystery of God is uttered to men through the word of preaching.

But knowledge is not the ultimate goal of the preaching of the word. We must delimit on two sides what is intended in the preaching of God's mighty acts. On the one hand it does not serve academic knowledge. It has been pointed out often enough that it is just in this point that the bible's understanding of the term "word" differs from the Greek understanding. If in Greek a content is communicated and made understandable so that it can be known, the bible uses "word" more in the sense of a salutation. In the Acts of the Apostles "the word '*didaskein*' [to teach, instruct], is used [in connection with *ho lógos*] in isolated cases (18:11; 15:35). This term must not be interpreted to mean the communication of theoretical knowledge. The word is determined in the first place not by the Greek use of the term, but far more from the Old Testament Jewish conceptions. . . . The word denotes therefore the communication of the content of a divine revelation, and is thus closely related with *euangelizesthai* [to preach, proclaim]."[130] Thus preaching does not give its report of the mighty acts of God as the communication of theoretic and academic knowledge. It is not intended to remain in the intellect as a wealth of knowledge, but to penetrate to the will so that a decision may be made concerning God's acts.

But we must also delimit the meaning of the communication of God's word through preaching from that form of practical knowledge which is simply pragmatic. This is that knowledge of the material world which man obtains without asking particularly whether he achieves it through his own research or whether he must have it communicated to him through instruction. But even when such instruction occurs through the efforts of a personal teacher it is still very different from God's revelation to men. For the instruction which imparts practical knowledge serves wholly the acquisition of the matter communicated: the personal instructor stands entirely in the background. The knowledge is obtained for the purpose of its profitable use in man's routine everyday life.

In the preaching of God's word another kind of communication takes place. The church's proclamation of the word of God allows the promulgation of the divine word itself to continue resounding. It has therefore no other meaning and purpose than the original promulgation itself. But God's word is not promulgated to men merely to communicate to them knowledge and science which would otherwise remain closed to them, or in order to make the exploitation of the world easier for them. When God communicates himself to men through his word he veils himself in this word and summons men under its covering to a personal decision so that they may now give themselves to him in response. This is intended to bring into being that life of fellowship which allows men to share mystically in the interior life of the triune God.

The Word as Proclamation

It is worthy of note that the New Testament displays a certain fondness for denoting the church's proclamation of the word of God as a message (*kerygma*). Of course teaching (*didache, didaskalia*) is also mentioned, but not in the sense of academic instruction with an assignment that must be learned. This is shown by the very fact that what is taught appears also as a way. Actually something is not taught which must be learned. Rather a direction is given in which one has to go. Even where the church's preaching has a teaching content it is directed toward the formation of life. That which is taught comes before men as a demand and a warning.

The church's homiletics, in distinguishing between the catechetical, teaching sermon and the consolatory, exhortatory sermon, does not intend any separation and exclusiveness. There is no teaching sermon which must not at the same time warn and demand as well. For its teaching speaks about God's revelation. And this always demands man's decisions, not merely in the sense of an assent in faith to the content of the teaching, but also in the sense of his yes to the consequence which what is taught has for the fashioning of his life. Conversely there is no exhortatory sermon which must not at the same time give instruction about what moral decision is demanded. It is of course quite impossible to be disposed to morally correct behavior unless one has been taught what moral demands are made. But the exhortative sermon must also teach, because the Christian's moral behavior can only be a response to what God has created and effected for man in the way of reality and a framework for his life. The sermon of exhortation must achieve its effective power less from the utterance of "thou shalt" and more from the motives which impel man to fulfill the moral demands made upon him. For Christian morality is not a code of arbitrary demands, but the logical consequence of the order of this world and of salvation as created by God and newly created by Christ. Man must of course fulfill his destiny as a creature made in the image of God primarily by administering the created world as one made in God's image, discerning in creation that order the world's creator has instituted as the order of his creation, and by following this order in his intercourse with all other creatures. The God who creates the world and man who administers it meet each other in their activity in creation. Nor is this principle abolished in the supernatural redemptive order of grace, but rather completed and carried out afresh in the face of sin. Thus the preaching of "thou shalt" must always be also the interpretation of "thou art"; and the preaching of the new life in Christ must also delineate the demands which determine human action.

Therefore the church's preaching is in all its forms *kerygma*, a herald's call, and a proclamation. This is easy to understand to some extent where the preaching church appears as the spokesman of God's sovereign rights. For in the church's preaching it is primarily the prophetical office of Christ which continues to be active. Through the church's word Christ appears before men as their king who rules over them and shows them the way. Christ's prophetic office is his kingly office because it is, needless to say, the sovereignty of the Father which Christ proclaims as the actual herald. He summons men who are intended to hear him and to follow him in the sacrifice he offers the Father for those who follow him. The church must continue this prophetic activity of Christ. The church's prophetic preaching is the continuation of the prophetic office of the exalted Christ.

In the preaching of the demands made by the moral law the church's kerygmatic, heraldic activity is quite directly and explicitly recognizable. But also in its teaching activity does the church's preaching exercise an heraldic office and bring forth its *kerygma*. Even when the preaching of the church tells of God's nature and activity it is never the bare communication of facts, but always direct address. The acceptance of this address through the faith of the hearers cannot be a noncommittal registration of information, but must produce readiness to behave in accordance with what has been accepted. "There is in the preaching of the gospel the continuation, in a certain sense, of its origin; for the same Jesus Christ who revealed himself in the gospel becomes publicly known through the gospel. This means first of all that in the gospel something 'concerning' or 'about' Jesus Christ is known through the gospel. . . . But such communications are not all that occurs in the preaching of the gospel, indeed this is not even the essential thing which happens in this connection. . . . What are we to say of the *Logos tes katallages* [word of reconciliation] (2 Cor 5:19) which God set alongside the cross as the other saving act? Is that merely a word which imparts knowledge of the reconciliation? And is the 'word of the cross' (1 Cor 1:18) only a word that teaches us about the cross? But how can this word be the power (*dynamis*) of God for those who are being saved? Does then the communication of knowledge save in the apostle Paul's sense? And is a sentence about the cross a means of God's power? . . . What does *keryssein ton logon* [to preach the word] mean in 2 Tim 4:2? It must certainly mean: to make the word resound by proclaiming it, to make it appear as the word. But then what does *keryssein ton Christon* [to preach Christ] mean? Does this too mean in the last analysis to make Christ present by proclaiming him? . . . The phrase in 1 Cor 6:20 *katangellein ton thanaton tou kyriou* certainly means: to proclaim the Lord's death and through this proclamation to make this death present. But then the phrase *ton Christon katangellein* (Phil 1:17; Col 1:28) also means nothing else than to proclaim Christ and thus through this proclamation and in this proclamation to make him present."[131] This view is further confirmed by the word of warning in the Didache (probably from the first half of the second century): "Day and night shalt thou think of him who preaches thee the word of God. For where his glory is preached, there is the Lord."[132]

The church's preaching imparts therefore, as *kergyma* and proclamation, not merely a content which must be learned, but brings this content somehow so strongly into the hearers' presence that they are drawn into the reality of the content—provided they hear the appeal of the proclamation and open themselves to the event it proclaims. But here, where we are still considering the efficacy of the preaching insofar as it communicates a definite content, we ought perhaps to speak less of the event which is proclaimed as being made present through its removal from its historical or other-worldly remoteness into the historical proximity of the believer in this world. Rather we should say that, conversely, the attentive believer who is prepared for a decision is drawn into the power of the event of which the proclamation speaks.

That is of course the characteristic feature of proclamation by means of a herald's cry. It is intended to cause the hearer to heed what is communicated, and to do so attentively and be prepared to obey; so that he allows himself to be drawn into the area of influence of the authority which the herald's proclamation asserts and of this authority's public power. And this is not merely something which occurred in earlier ages when the herald's message proclaimed a communication of the ruler or his personal presence. The same thing takes place today in the simple proclamation of an official regulation through the town crier in a village, through a public notice, or through radio and television. The event made known or the regulation of official authority with its proclaimed will penetrate into the presence of him to whom the proclamation is addressed, and he comes under the sway of the power here proclaimed.

So too the message of the church's preaching of God's word is not a noncommittal disclosure of an unknown reality. Naturally the reality which is preached is often not so unknown as to make it necessary to speak of it continually. Nevertheless repeated preaching does have a real point, and not merely in the pedagogical sense, in that repetition is the mother of knowledge. The point of repeated preaching is that through it the substance of salvation is proclaimed ever afresh before men, and in this way they are brought under the sway of the mighty acts of salvation, with all that that implies for men's salvation. This is intended to promote not better knowledge of the substance of preaching, but rather living contact with it.

2 The Efficacy of the Preaching Message

The effectual preaching of God's word by the church is a many-sided phenomenon. This should be taken properly into consideration in attempting to interpret the part played by preaching in the church's redemptive work. Quite apart from the fact that this phenomenon is so much a part of the secret inner realm of the church which Christ founded to be the vessel of divine activity that human attempts at interpretation very soon reach their limits, it is probably the case that of the various attempts at interpretation which are made, one person tries to throw light on one side and another person on another side of the total phenomenon. Thus they need not exclude one another; they must, rather, complement each other.

Now when we attempt to explain *how* the preaching of God's word, so far as it is considered under the aspect of a content which is preached, can be effectual, then we must proceed from the question of *what* it is that preaching is supposed to effect.

Faith as an Effect of Preaching

The question what the church's preaching is supposed to arouse and effect in its hearers can be answered very briefly with the single word: faith. Paul has said this very clearly. In the passage referred to, the question of why preaching exists and for what purpose is not raised however. So we raise the question here. We assume the existence of the preaching of God's word in the church and wish to know what its goal and purpose are. In the passage from the Epistle to the Romans which we have in mind here the opposite is the case. There it is assumed that a certain effect is to be achieved, namely the salvation of men by faith. The question is raised: in what manner is this salvation through human faith to be attained? The answer: through the preaching of the church, which sends out its messengers that they may preach God's word in the strength of the church's mission and thus effect faith and men's salvation. "Every one who calls upon the name of the Lord will be saved. But how are men to call upon him in whom they have not believed? And how are they to believe in him whom they have never heard? And how are they to hear without a preacher? And how can men preach unless they are sent? . . . So faith comes from what is heard, and what is heard comes by the preaching of Christ" (Rom 10:13–17).

The passage displays so intimate and exclusive a connection between salvation through faith and preaching of God's word in the strength of the church's sending that it is also possible to reverse the statement. It is not only true that the attainment of salvation in faith presupposes the preaching of the word of God; but conversely as well, the preaching of God's word serves salvation by awaking faith in men. The preaching of God's word by the church is actually a judgment which divides men, because not all men allow the preaching to take effect in their lives. Men are divided into believers and nonbelievers through the different positions they take up in response to the preaching through which God's word comes to them. "But they have not all heeded the gospel; for Isaiah says: 'Lord, who has believed what he has heard from us?' (Is 33:1)" (Rom 10:16).

Therefore those men who as members of the church allow themselves to be touched by the church's message and who participate actively in the church's life are called the faithful. Faith as such is certainly not the whole of Christian life. But it is at least its beginning. For Christian life can exist only where God has begun to visit man and to touch him. Of course Christian life is brought into being by man in free decision. But this freedom does not mean that man has the initiative. His own deed must always be a decision about a divine word of salutation which has already occurred. This salutation takes place in a word God addresses to man. In the general preaching of the church God communicates himself to each individual hearer and believer. The decision he makes about this divine word which goes forth makes man a believer or an unbeliever. This decision is however not merely a single yes which man utters here and now to what is said to him. What is said to him there stands in a very living connection with a whole host of redemptive acts and divine demands which are present in the life of the church. Therefore life in this church and the fashioning of man's own life according to the directions of God which are laid up in the church is that response of faith which is intended to be called forth as an effect of preaching.

But how are we to conceive of this faith as being effected by the church's preaching of the word? Faith is really not a particularly simple thing. This is shown even by the history of the church's proclamation of the faith and of the embroiled controversies over misunderstandings and erroneous doctrines. The Reformation of the sixteenth century determined what faith is in a manner different from that of the Catholic church. But even Catholic attempts to interpret what faith is display certain differences of emphasis. And if we consult the sources from which the revealing God allows us to know what faith actually is, then the matter is by no means so clear as the simple word "faith" would lead us to believe. Holy scripture seems to mean by faith something more comprehensive and diverse than does, for instance, modern theology. But even within the framework of holy scripture faith does not appear by any means everywhere in the same form. How are we to explain this observation?

Faith is not unlike the consumption of food. The process of eating is in itself comparatively simple. But when food is consumed by eating something begins which goes far beyond this simple process. The food is really consumed in the process of metabolism. And what happens in metabolism is a highly differentiated structure of events and effects which are all still the consumption of food, and yet which can still be distinguished for consumption. Now what is it in this whole diverse process of assimilation which is eating? It can hardly be disputed that the answer to this question is in large part a matter of convention, of arbitrary definition and delimitation of terms. It is legitimate to say that eating means only the immediate taking of food into the mouth and stomach. But if we wish, we can, in speaking of eating, mean also the further process of metabolism, the assimilation of the food in the eater's organism. What is actually meant will, when necessary, have to be explicitly stated if we do not want to talk at cross purposes.

Something similar may be true with regard to faith. Without doubt it is legitimate to limit the concept of faith at first to that act in which the reality God has revealed to man is received as true and assented to because God has revealed it. In this case faith proceeds directly from that organ of man's intellectual life which is responsible for the reception of truth, namely the understanding. In an age in which men are only too happy to put aside religious statements as presumptions which commit man to nothing, or as mythological notions, it is in fact extraordinarily important to emphasize especially this feature of faith as oriented toward objective reality and truth—though it is also true that this feature cannot and should not stand alone. The acceptance of revealed truth occurs, in fact, not for its own sake, but for the sake of the encounter with God who utters himself in revelation, and to make it possible for man to fashion his life in answering devotion to God. We believe the *truth* God has revealed because we believe the *testimony* of this revealing God, and because we believe with devotion *in God* who in revelation communicates himself. Therefore in terms of the concrete reality of human existence this affirmation of the understanding, which is faith in the narrower sense, alone and in isolation from everything else, simply does not exist. It exists only in combination with the decision of the will and a life fashioned according to this truth which is accepted. Genuine intellectual faith never exists without spreading out at once into the will, temperament and entire attitude and life of a living man. Faith is the act in which the understanding accepts the truth. Therefore it is always performed by the whole man: it grows out of man's total attitude and behavior and has a reciprocal effect upon his attitude and behavior.

This diversity displayed in the concrete, living act of faith affects of course the use of the term "faith." When we speak of faith do we mean only the intellectual act which accepts God's revelation as true? Do we mean by faith the individual decision for or against God made afresh by each individual? Or do we mean the total attitude of a life bearing the Christian stamp, on the basis of which this life is made continually fresh? In point of fact, we may never employ the word "faith" in one of these senses to the exclusion of the other.

Now when we say that man's faith is summoned and effected by the preaching of God's word, we are looking at man who is summoned as a concrete, living phenomenon; and we are considering faith in its total complexity, as it actually is. When someone considers to be true what God has revealed he is hearing God's word, in the first place, against the background of a total human disposition. But in this intellectual assent to revelation not only the man's liveliness of temperament but also the will's trust and love are aroused. And this summons him to fashion his life in accordance with the dictates of his mind, as moved by faith. The faith aroused by the preaching of God's word is something complex. Its individual elements do not simply exist loosely, side by side with each other. Rather are they bound up organically with one another and condition or cause each other. Precisely here are essential clues for the answer to our question how the content of preaching brings faith into being.

Preparatory Efficacy

Two things are now established. The Christian life of faith—and by this we mean the life determined by God's word in Christ—is something which is worked out in the world in the fashioning of the whole of life. Christian life is not limited to the times of explicit divine worship. It is not compressed into the times when man listens to the preaching of God's word and responds to this preaching by joining in the celebration of the church's worship. On the contrary, what is Christian has consequences in all the dimensions, times and activities of man's life or it is nothing. The life which is so fashioned, and which must be brought into being ever anew, must prove the reality of its Christian name. And this it does in a way similar to that of an effect indicating its cause—a cause which asserts its reality through its efficacy.

But another point is established as well. This Christian life which is thus effected is caused in some way or other by the preaching of God's word. Because the believer has heard God's word through the church's preaching his life is fashioned in a Christian manner. His life is the effect of his hearing of God's word in preaching. Thus Paul thanks God continually for the fact that the Thessalonians have received the word of his preaching as God's word, and also for the fact—and this above all—that this word is then at work in the believers. This efficacy of the word goes so far that the Thessalonians, by allowing their lives to be fashioned by the word and thus to become a testimony for the word, have come into opposition with their countrymen similar to that experienced by Paul with his Jewish countrymen (1 Th 2:13–16).

It cannot be doubted that there exists between preaching on the one hand and the effectually fashioned human life on the other a living, causal connection. The preaching of God's word is not only the occasion on which Christians begin to fashion their lives differently from the way they have fashioned them before. Rather they fashion their lives afresh and differently because the word of God has been preached, and in the form demanded by the content of this preaching. The preaching of God's word is the genuine cause of man's fashioning his life anew and making of it a Christian life.

It is vital now to explain what this causal connection

looks like. For no matter how clear it sounds when we speak of cause and effect, the matter still needs clarification. There are various kinds of causality. It is important to notice this in our context for the simple reason that the attempt is often made to distinguish the efficacy of the sacrament from the preaching of God's word according to two kinds of causality. Such attempts run somewhat as follows: the sacrament imparts the grace of the Christian life immediately and directly according to the pattern of an actual, physical cause. The preaching of the word on the other hand works upon man's decisions only by influencing him mentally and morally. It thus disposes him for the reception of grace. But the cause of grace is not preaching but something else. What is positively stated in this distinction is not to be doubted. The sacrament is really the instrumental cause of grace and of man's justification.[133] And the preaching of God's word does, in fact, work upon man morally and through its intent, so that he may allow himself to be moved through the content of what is said to the free decision to try and fashion his life according to the Christian pattern. The question is simply whether this is everything that can be said on both sides. It cannot be denied that the sacrament has, along with its instrumental and causal effect, the intentional and instrumental effect which is proper to the sign and to the word. Therefore in the case of the preaching of God's word its intentional and moral mode of action at least does not necessarily exclude another, effective mode of action. But it is not unimportant to ascertain first of all how the preaching of God's word works upon man morally, by its intention, through rousing him to decision and disposing him rightly.

This mode of operation is, first of all, proper to the word as such. What psychology says about the significance of the word in respect to the flood of worldly events applies here for the portrayal and actual presentation here and now of God's redemptive work in past history through the word of preaching. "The world which is addressed in the word is quite truly the ascertained and established world. The inarticulate experience of the animal is exhausted in fleeting impressions which vary from moment to moment. The animal is itself a wave in the flood of events in which nothing is fixed and enduring. It is just this which changes in man's case, as soon as he discovers the word. In the word man calls a halt to the stream of impressions. In addressing the world through the word the impressions are arranged according to permanent groups of meaning and are brought before the consciousness as something concrete that a man can survey and by which he can orient himself. . . . The word is the symbol of that which is permanent in the flood of appearances. In it the fleetingness of these apearances is halted."[134] So also in the word of preaching the flood of historical redemptive events is grasped and brought before man for his decision. Again and again men are addressed in preaching and moved to fashion their lives in accordance with what is said. This all remains true, even if we should find that preaching also has a mode of operation similar to that of the sacrament. How does the word come to be efficacious in the human listener? When man listens the content which is communicated by the word is first of all brought before his mind. Since the truth which is accepted is not intended merely to be recognized so that it may simply be registered mentally, but is a reality in the communication of which God himself presents himself to man as one who loves and effects salvation, man's will must react: the will must evaluate this loving attention of God and respond to it. Man must for his part fashion a life which expresses devotion to God and thus shows his response to be to a certain degree as real as the word.

In this way therefore the preaching of God's word does not immediately effect divine grace. Rather the preaching first of all communicates God's redemptive will, and appeals to man to open and to prepare himself for the actual self-communication of God in grace. What is achieved through the content of preaching is not yet the divine life itself but man's readiness to receive this life. This is, to be sure, the indispensable prerequisite for God's life-giving entrance into man,[135] but it is not yet the actual state of grace. We can also say that this condition of openness and of devotion to God which is prepared in man through the preaching of God's word is the material cause of salvation; and this material cause is then elevated to the condition of an actually sanctified human being through the life of God, who penetrates man so completely that he dwells in him and thus becomes the formal cause of his salvation. Since the preparation of the material cause occurs at least in part through the preaching of God's word, this preaching has already a large share in the origin of the state of grace in man, although the actual formal cause of justification is not yet present. A question we will have to consider separately however is whether the actual event of the church's preaching of God's word also plays an active part in this connection, that is, whether the preaching of God's word in the church is not merely the preparation of the material cause of salvation but also, in unity with the sacraments, bestows the formal cause of man's salvation.

Before we pass on to this question let us point out how important is the proper effort of the preacher to find a good, persuasive and moving form for his words, if what we have said is to be realized. Everything we may have to say later about a quasi-sacramental efficacy of the actual event of preaching cannot replace the preacher's efforts or render them unimportant. The preacher who is by nature unskilled or who is too burdened with other tasks may of course be tempted to put his trust too much in the idea that the simple reading of the gospel works like a sacrament, and that his efforts over his sermon are therefore not particularly necessary.

Such a view must be characterized as untenable. Even if it could be established that the preaching of God's word, whether in the reading of the words of the bible or in a humanly composed sermon, shares in the objective efficacy of the sacraments' mediation of grace, the actual application of this efficacy is still dependent upon the assertion of the disposing power of the word which is preached. For even the efficacy of the sacraments *ex opere operato* excludes from the *opus operantis* only the "*ex*": in other words, it does not deny man's own personal efforts as the meritorious cause of grace. But this does not say that the sacrament is also effective where there is no *opus operantis,* no personal effort on the part of the human recipient to dispose himself properly. And to bring about this personal effort and proper disposition is of course the special task of the well preached content of the sermon.

3 Preaching as an Event which Effects Grace

Holy scripture testifies in a way that cannot be overlooked that "the word of God is living and active" (Heb 4:12). The explanation for this fact is to be found first of all in the moving power of the content which the human mind takes from preaching and allows to work upon the will and the temperament. Seen in this light the preaching of God's word is distinguished from human words only by the fact that it is things revealed by God which are presented and made effectual in preaching. God's revelation sinks into man's thinking and planning and stamps his decisions with human and this-worldly knowledge. Through this combination of divine revelation and human knowledge man's existence already attains to a certain extent a divine and human form. But here there is only an indirect efficacy for grace. What happens directly is that the content of the preaching and the manner in which this content is presented make man open for God, though of course even this does not happen without the work of divine grace.

We are compelled inwardly now to pose the question whether the preaching of God's word does not also work as an efficient cause on the state of grace itself. Does the preaching of God's word continue to have only an indirect and preparatory significance for the bestowal of grace upon man? Or does preaching also share really and effectively in the origin of man's justification and sanctification—in a manner similar to, or in connection with, the causal efficacy of the sacraments?

1 The Question and its Meaning

It must be admitted at the outset that the answer we think we shall find in revelation to the question we have posed does not really seem at first sight to mean too much. For it will be shown that the sermon's significance does indeed go beyond that preparatory effect and indirect preparation for grace of which we spoke immediately above, but that a genuine efficacy for grace exclusive to the sermon and separate from that of the sacrament cannot be ascribed to preaching. But if preaching has such an efficacy only through its connection with, and orientation toward, the reception of the sacraments, then that does not seem to contribute really very much toward the interpretation of the church's preaching. We must therefore say something first of all about what this finding can mean nevertheless. And in this connection we must establish boundaries on both sides, so as to prevent the danger of saying too little as well as the danger of saying too much.

Two Points of Departure

We must first of all establish once again two findings we have already reached as points of departure. Only if both are borne in mind simultaneously will it be seen that our question does lead beyond what we have discussed up to this point in a meaningful manner, and yet not so far beyond as to forfeit the proper mutual relationship between the functions of the church's life.

The first of these findings arises from a comparison of the two preceding sections with one another. In the section immediately preceding, the efficacy of the preaching of God's word was traced to its content and to the humanly effective manner in which this content is presented; and this efficacy of preaching was seen to have an indirect effect upon the attainment of justification. Man allows himself to be made the vessel into which God can pour himself as a sanctifying gift. This preparation is not yet santification and justification but merely the preliminary groundwork for them. And the preparation of man is not a meritorious cause which would compel God to give his grace. But such preparation does stand under God's promise, given once for all time, that he will not refuse to come and take up his abode with him who with the help of God's effectual grace prepares himself as a vessel through listening to the preaching of God's word. "If a man loves me, he will keep my word." Such a man has heard the word of the Lord preached and stands open for its further development: "And we will come to him and make our home with him" (Jn 14:23). On the basis of this promise of our Lord it is certain that God will bestow himself in justifying grace and sanctification upon the human heart which has been prepared through the moral efficacy of preaching. It is no less certain than the production of an effect by its cause when the cause is properly applied. And yet the certainty in this case is not based on the relationship of cause and effect, but on God's promise, which makes absolutely certain that when the disposing condition has been fulfilled the promise will become effective. Or, if we wish to employ the concept of causality here as well, we may not speak of an efficient cause, but—at least in an analogous sense—of a material cause prepared through the moral action of the preaching of God's word, which in turn produces a personal decision and an act of divine grace. In this way God himself can then, as a kind of formal cause, penetrate such a man to justify and sanctify him.

Let us now compare what we found in the first section of this second part, where no further effort at more profound interpretation was made, to be testified to by holy scripture as the actual result of effectual preaching of God's word. It then appears that we are justified in claiming that this preaching has a moral influence on the mind and will, disposing them for sanctification: indeed this claim cannot be relinquished. But this does not exhaust the statements of the New Testament. If it is true that expressions like "word of life," "word of grace," "word of reconciliation" and "word of salvation" do not merely mean that something is said about life, grace, reconciliation and salvation, then this additional meaning can only be that the proclamation of the word imparts life, grace, reconciliation and salvation. "The preaching of the word which occurs 'in the name' of Christ, that is, in obedience to his command and with his authority . . . is precisely the '*logos des kyrios,*' the word spoken by our Lord himself after he has been transfigured in the Spirit (Acts 8:25; 12:24; 19:20). Indeed it is Christ himself who appears and works in the *kerygma* in verbal or bodily form (Acts 10:36–38; 20:32). Hence the word is really God's word (1 Th 2:13), and the power of God to those who believe and are being saved (1 Cor 1:18; Rom 1:16)."[136]

There is in the New Testament a remarkable parallelism between God's word and his work which makes the two really interchangeable, so that they must be to some extent equivalent. God's work is always his word as well, the salutation he addresses to man, appealing to his mind and to the decision of his will. And conversely God's word is always his work as well, effecting grace in him who hears the word and receives it. "So Jesus said: 'When you have lifted up the Son of man, then you will know that I am he, and that I *do* nothing on my own authority but *speak* thus as the Father taught me' " (Jn 8:28). "The words that I say to you I do not *speak* on my own authority; but the Father who dwells in me *does* his works" (Jn 14:10). "If I had not come and *spoken* to them, they would not have sin; but now they have no excuse for their sin. . . . If I had not *done* among them the works which no one else did, they would not have sin; but now they have seen and hated both me and my Father" (Jn 15:22,24). Therefore our Lord's word and his work really stand for one another. And similarly in the Old Testament God's word seems to be really identical in meaning with his work and interchangeable with work in a way similar to that which we have observed in these johannine texts. "The word of the Lord is upright; and all his work is done in faithfulness" (Ps 33 [32]:4). In view of the stylistic parallelism of semitic poetry, these words can only mean that uprightness and faithfulness are equivalent in meaning—and word and work as well. "The Lord is faithful in all his words, and gracious in all his works" (Ps 145 [144]:14).

Salvation, man's justification, is without any doubt the work of God. But this work or effect is ascribed to God's word as it lives in the mouth of the church's preaching. It is of course true that the functions of the church's life sometimes make God's word, sometimes his work, more visible, and this in various ways and with varying effectiveness. Therefore there is no doubt that in the sacraments God's redemptive work is more immediately and effectively portrayed, insofar as this redemptive work has its climax in Christ's redeeming sacrifice; whereas in the preaching of God's word it is more directly his word which appears and takes shape. But here too we can say: where God's work appears it is at the same time his word. And where the word of God resounds in the church it is also his work. But God's work implies efficacy, and what it effects is grace.

Hence our first observation is that according to the evidence of holy scripture the preaching of God's word seems to effect more than the psychological and moral motivation of man by means of knowledge and the appeal to the will which is proper to all human words. More than that, God's word as it is preached in the church seems to cooperate in producing, effectually and in fact, man's state of grace, his righteousness and his salvation. "The word of the preacher is God's word. God makes use of these words of the priest which sound upon the ear in order to speak himself in every man's ear and soul. This word of preaching thus becomes in God's hands the instrument which somehow effects in the hearer that which it says. With the outer word of the church's servant God joins the inner word of his Spirit. Thus he touches the understanding and heart of the hearer and, if the hearer willingly receives the word, God makes it fruitful in him . . . Thus this external preaching of God's word to generation after generation accomplishes the mystery of Christ and the mystery of salvation which the Father works in man through Christ in the Holy Spirit."[137]

At the same time however we must hold with equal insistence to the fact that the sacraments instituted by Christ are the instrumental cause and source of the grace of justification. And that because they portray in their own right and make present that event in which the grace of justification was earned for us, namely Christ's sacrifice on the cross. As symbols the sacramental acts point to Christ's sacrifice, which is the actual source of our salvation. And as symbols of this special, sacramental kind they do not merely point to Christ's sacrifice, but make it mystically but at the same time really present for man who stands in need of salvation. Thus we are to come into contact with Christ's sacrifice in a human and bodily manner. This contact is the active, personal act of man. By having the sacrament administered to him man goes and enters into contact with the sacrifice offered by Christ, affirming it in his free decision as his own sacrifice. At the same time however man is the one who is laid hold of in this process. For in the most essential element of the event he is passive. Man cannot accomplish the actual decisive element, but only Christ who, as head of the human race and because of his dignity as a divine person, can offer a sacrifice which is certain to be accepted by God. If man is to be accepted with his sacrifice he must be drawn into Christ's sacrificial act in order to be taken up in this act to the Father on high. What man can do himself however is no little amount. He can and must allow himself to be taken up by entering into that sacramental form which has been given to Christ's sacrifice so that it may be present in the church. That which effects the grace of justification is thus Christ's sacrifice insofar as it is made present in its ecclesiastical form through the veil of the sacrament. This efficacy can be ascribed to the sacrament to the degree in which it is the tangible veil and vessel of Christ's sacrifice. Here then is the reason why the sacraments are the source of man's justification, whether it be achieved for the first time, or augmented, or even won again after having been lost.

There is only one other thing which, to some degree, comes into question as a source of salvation alongside the sacraments, or aside from them. In reality however this is not something parallel to or outside the sacrament, but what the Council of Trent, in line with theological tradition, calls the desire (*votum*) for the sacrament.[138]

If this is true, then the preaching of God's word cannot be an instrumental cause for the grace of justification alongside of the seven sacramental signs. If the preaching of the word of God really shares in the causality of man's salvation through justifying grace, then this can be true, at most, in the manner which applies also in the case of desire for the sacrament. Only if the preaching of God's word is understood as in some sense a part of the sacrament, or as an act oriented toward the sacrament so that it contains some of the sacrament's efficacy through emanation or anticipation, does preaching seem to play an effectual role in the origin of justifying grace.

Preaching as Part of a Whole

But in this case the importance of the question as to the actual efficacy of the sermon does seem to become somewhat questionable. If the efficient causality which gives to the preaching of the word a new redemptive role does not after all pertain to preaching in and of itself, then it seems that this causality does not actually belong to preaching at all; and the discussion seems to be an argument about nothing. If we ask what the preaching of God's word as such and in its own right effects, then it seems that we must deny to it any sacramental efficacy for grace, since any other answer would impair the Catholic belief with regard to the sacraments. The preaching of God's word does not have as an organ of the church's mediation of grace the same relationship to the sacraments as the individual sacraments have to one another. They stand, although not without certain limitations, side by side as differing organs of salvation. This is still true even if the view of a number of theologians is correct that there is in the last analysis but one single sacramental source of grace, the eucharist. All the other sacraments are, according to this view, oriented toward the eucharist, and it is from the eucharist in virtue of this orientation that they possess their efficacy for grace. Moreover in the other sacraments a kind of desire for the eucharist is realized objectively; hence the eucharist is efficacious in the other sacraments.[139] Even if this view is correct—and it is, in fact, disputed—the individual sacraments still remain in some sense sources of grace which stand side by side. And at any rate this is a different relationship from the one which prevails between the preaching of the word and the sacraments. In this case however it does not seem as if we have come very far in establishing as effective a role for preaching in the mediation of salvation.

Now the importance of our question does not lie in the wish to ascribe under all circumstances to the church's preaching of the word of God an efficient causality of its own, independent from that of the sacrament. In this way neither the significance of the sacrament nor that of the sermon would at all appear in their full and proper light. The tendency of our question is certainly not to place sermon and sacrament in some way side by side as alternatives, and to offer the member of the church, as it were, a choice between them. Rather our question and its corresponding answer are important precisely for the reason that it is possible to show by means of this example how the functions of the church's life must be forged again into that unity which belongs to them as the portrayal of Christ's redemptive work—which in its own turn must be discovered as a double unity. The analytical work of scholarship is good and necessary just as long as it is understood as operating in the service of the deeper knowledge of the whole. But if scholarly analysis pushes so far into the foreground that it forgets or loses the synthesis of its individual statements, then it must be called to order. "The command of the present time is synthesis,"[140] not in opposition to analysis, but as its continuation and as the determination of its goal. The analytical tendency has perhaps shown itself to be fateful in this question. For when an effect is accomplished by a complex total action it is quite legitimate to try to analyze this complex action in order to recognize it in itself and in its immanent structure. But if we pose the question of the relationship of this action to what lies outside of it —which is also the question as to how such an action exercises its effect—then we must consider the action in its total complexity. It is impossible to pose the question with regard to each partial element of the action in the same way as it is posed with regard to the whole. In this point the reality of complex causality possesses a certain imperfect similarity to the triune God himself. In his divine immanence God exists in three persons. But in his causative, creative work outside of himself he is a single principle.[141] The act of creation cannot be ascribed to one of the three persons alone to the exclusion of the others.

We have therefore, strictly speaking, no obligation at all to pursue the question whether or not the church's preaching of the word of God unfolds an efficacy for grace of its own. The question is rather whether that efficacy for grace we are accustomed without much thought to ascribe to the sacraments alone does not in reality belong to the sacraments in active unity with the preaching of the word, the two together constituting a dual, though unified cause. The fact that this efficacy is nevertheless attributed to the sacraments by way of simplification can then be justified by the consideration that it is, of course, only when the sacraments are administered that this duality of the effective elements—the preaching of the word and administration of the sacraments, administration of the sacraments accompanied by preaching of the word—has reached its visible conclusion.

2 Preaching as an Image and Sign

The preaching of God's word is linked and related to the sacraments at least by the fact that they are both essential functions of the church's life. The sacraments are not merely the efficient cause of salvation. They are not instruments whose form is immaterial provided merely that they are applied. They are no less signs than causes. We may presume something similar, but in a greater degree, with regard to the preaching of God's word. For the word is always a sign as well and hence a statement concerning, and pointing to, a hidden reality. This fact, that the efficacy of preaching and sacrament is never exercised without signification and declaration, indeed that it is linked with these, is founded upon the further fact that these actions bring the church itself into being. The visible, social reality of the church is a sacramental image and sign of the invisible kingdom of God, of the life of fellowship with God in grace; and the church contains within itself both actually and effectually this reality it signifies. From this essential fact in the church's being, and from the tasks that result from it, we must therefore take our departure.

Christ's Saving Work in the Vessel of the Church

If the church has been founded by Christ as the continuation of his saving word, then it must be a corporal reality, penetrated by God; and in those actions of the church which stem from its essential nature Christ's saving work must be set forth. The church's institutional, and thus in a sense static nature is all too apt to tempt us to be content with the conception that the fruits of a past saving work are stored up somewhere or other, and that the church has the job of distributing them. This conception is however too simple to be free from possible danger. We must not overlook the great inaccuracy which is present in this picture of the church. The First Vatican Council did not say that it is merely the fruits of Christ's work which are to be interpreted statically, which are stored up permanently in the church; it said that the dynamism of the work itself continues in the church.[142] This can only mean that this work actually occurs in the church's life.

The mystery of the church contains in the essential functions of its life Christ's work stored up through its portrayal in images, signs and symbols. In this symbolic manner, which cannot be dissolved by human explanation, Christ's work is made present once again. Thus the church helps to make Christ's saving work actually present not merely by causing men through its teaching and exhortation to present an open heart to the Lord and giver of grace. The church does indeed do this too through its preaching of God's word of revelation and exhortation. But to see the church's work and its preaching of God's word only under this aspect would be to subject the mystery of the church to a naturalistic curtailment. As necessary as teaching and exhortation are to prepare the faithful for the reception of the sacraments and of the grace which proceeds from them, they still remain to some extent exterior to the actual bestowal of grace. If this were all that the church had to accomplish for man's sanctification and justification, we could quite well suppose that the mature man, properly prepared, could find his way to an encounter with God quite as well without the church's efforts. And the goal of the church's work would then necessarily be to make itself more and more superfluous.

Such a view however must either lead to the conclusion that the church's energetic work, which does not arouse the impression of seeking to make itself superfluous, is a presumptuous intrusion between God and the individual; or else it must lead to the recognition that beyond activity of this kind the church's work must have a deeper meaning which does not render the work superfluous, even when man no longer seems to need teaching and exhortation. Only if the church is the very embodiment of salvation can we explain properly the dogged perseverance with which the church pursues man even when he thinks he can find his way by himself.

Nor can we do justice to the mystery of the church by that other conception of its work which is so natural in an age when man has brought the world so largely under his control and administration. It is said that the church "administers" the sacraments and the word of God. This manner of speaking has even entered into the church's theological textbooks.[143] Inasmuch as the visible side of the church does have the character of a social phenomenon this manner of speaking is certainly not simply false. But it does not exhaust the matter. The social aspect is not the whole of the church's meaning and nature. Founded as a society, the church is beyond itself or, in its hidden depths, a sign which points to something else. In turning our gaze therefore upon the social church we must allow ourselves to be led in the direction this sign points out to, into the still incomplete but already present inner realm of God's kingly rule. Therefore the conception of the church's administration of the sacraments and of the word is only very provisionally correct. If the minister of the sacraments were really only the administrator of a juridically valid process, then the efficacy of the sacrament could be considered something quite magical, separate from the personal action of man. The person of the minister would become quite unimportant. We would no longer see the minister as portraying the God-man who, according to the ancient conviction, is the actual minister of the sacraments.

Men do not come to the God of their salvation by passing by the church but by entering the church. For the church is the corporal and historical form of salvation. In the church is the realization of something expressed by the Council of Trent with regard to the sacraments when it calls them "the visible form of invisible grace."[144] The Christ who has ascended into the invisible realms and who is men's salvation insofar as they are received into living union with him through the Holy Spirit has surrounded himself with the church as with a vicarious body. By being incorporated into this visible body of Christ man shares in the inner life of his body which is righteousness, grace and life for men. The church does not actually mediate salvation to men by giving away salvation. The church accomplishes in its visible and human veil that historically past or other-worldly and distant salvation which is Christ in his work—the work that "follows" him (see Ap 14:13) in his glory. And through the exercise of its vital functions the church makes this salvation present and allows men to share in it.

Thus this mystery of the church consists in the fact that the church is not a final reality in itself, but an image and sign of the actual reality; and its signification displays that realism which is proper to the sacraments. The church is a figurative reality, a sign, in which the salvation it signifies is portrayed in human fashion and made tangible. This is the basis of a certain ambivalence in the church. The church must insist that membership in its ranks is necessary for salvation. But this claim does not actually have its foundation in the church itself, as if the church were itself the final goal to be attained in the process of salvation. The visible church is an image and sign of that salvation which possesses in the church a visible and symbolic corporality. Thus the church points beyond itself. An image or sign fails to fulfill its essential purpose if it holds the observer fixed in itself. In the church this relative, indicative character has two dimensions. It appears first in the church's eschatological preaching. The church knows that it is oriented toward the kingdom of God at the end of time. Into this kingdom the church must lead its members through the dissolution of its own earthly form at the end of the world. But because this eschatological reality is already contained in the visible church like an invisible soul, the visible church points to its own inner depths. The life of the church's fellowship which is lived in the bodily form is effective for salvation only when it is a sign which portrays a hidden inner life with and in God. One can speak of different levels, though a number of theologians are not fond of the term, because they fear that the close connection of these so-called levels will not be properly understood.[145] It is also possible to use the figure of the living unity of body and soul in man and to speak of the body and soul of the church, thus portraying the unity of the life of the church's visible fellowship as the body, and the invisible grace of Christ in the Holy Spirit that is hidden within the church as its soul. Or we can speak also of the fellowship of the church as the sacramental sign which signifies the kingdom of God that is hidden within the church. What is meant in each case is that the church, though absolutely necessary to salvation, is a symbolic and figurative signpost pointing to an invisible, inner reality. The real kingdom of God and of his grace is portrayed and made present in the visible church.

That the church has from its beginning thought of itself in this way is shown above all by its belief with regard to the sacraments. Thus an ancient tradition interprets baptism as that sacrament through which man, who is struggling not to sink in the flood, is seized and incorporated into the church as into a saving ark. But if the church is interpreted as the ark, that can only mean that safety and salvation are kept in readiness in its visible structure for those who are struggling not to sink in the flood. The church has always understood its assembly for the fellowship of the eucharist as an anticipated portrayal of the eternal marriage feast. Thomas Aquinas takes up an ancient Christian tradition when he interprets the eucharistic meal in its double aspect as the portrayal of the past death of Christ and of the future eternal life as symbolized by the heavenly banquet.[146] The sacrament of penance admits the sinner once more into the church's eucharistic fellowship from which his sin had excluded him. And this readmittance into the peace of the church is the earnest and portrayal of the newly recovered peace with God.

But we shall understand correctly how the visible church through its character as a sign and image portrays the invisible grace of God only if we see this signification as possessing a realism which sets it apart from the images we meet in everyday life. These are connected with the reality they portray merely because they recall this reality. The contact between the observer and the portrayed reality is occasioned through the image, it is true; but it is realized subjectively only through the power of man's memory and desire.

In the image of salvation which the church and its vital functions present this is also the case, to be sure. In the mutual relationship of the spiritual office with the lay community the church portrays figuratively the inter-relationship between the incarnate redeemer and humanity which is in need of redemption. And when the believer has the word of God preached to him and the sacrament administered to him by the priest he is supposed to be reminded that Christ has become man and has died a sacrificial death in order to bring God to us and us to God. But this image is more than a mere portrayal for the purpose of recollection. It is not only man's memory and desire which are intended to bridge the chasm between history and the other world. The bridge has long since been thrown across this chasm, for the church and its essential life do in fact contain in a mysterious manner the work of redemption they portray. When man in his mind and will remembers the past or other-worldly redemptive event because of its figurative and symbolic portrayal, he comes into contact with the very reality and efficacy of this event which has mysteriously overcome the chasm of history through being preserved in the vessel of the church and of its activity. The work Christ performed in our history has of course become trans-historical as well; in his resurrection and ascension Christ's work has been made continually present before the eternal God. Thus this work, having now been freed from historical ties, can be offered in tangible form to historical men in the images and signs Christ has instituted. This is a mystery, but it is not impossible.

The Church's Preaching as a Sign of Salvation

Now the preaching of God's word is a substantial part of this sign of salvation which the church is. Seen institutionally and statically the church is indeed an image of the salvation which has been achieved in Christ. For the fact that in the church a spiritual office and ministry stands confronting the community reminds us, prior to any action, that salvation occurred by Christ's coming to men and leading them in his sacrifice to the Father. But that is of course not the end of the matter. In the polar structure which is part of its institution the church possesses an inner dynamism in virtue of which a living movement back and forth links the two poles with one another. And this is a continuation of the connection between Christ and the disciples.

The preaching of the word of God is an essential part of this continuance of Christ's redemptive work through signs and symbols. This statement is really not surprising since of course every word, sign and image is the portrayal of what it speaks about. This is the way, in fact, in which the word or sign fulfills its purpose between men who wish to communicate with one another. Because man cannot take in hand the reality about which he wants to make a communication and give it to the other, he seizes it vicariously in an image or in a word. The word takes the intellectual content from the reality, its meaning and peculiarity, in order to communicate these to him to whom the man speaks. The word portrays the reality, and is therefore a kind of sign or image of the reality. The word is an image and sign of this kind because its substance contains something of the reality and communicates this reality vicariously. The actual act of speaking in which the word is imparted does not stand in the foreground here, but is entirely in the service of the imparted substance.

In our present context however we are concerned with another kind of symbolic effect of the preaching of God's word. We are investigating not the content which is preached and which can embrace the entire range of redemptive activity, but rather the fact and act of preaching itself. Though the content and act of preaching are indeed indivisible they are still not identical: and they can each have their own kind of symbolism and efficacy.

What is meant here is familiar to us to some extent in the case of the sacraments. There the symbolic meaning of the content can be very clearly distinguished from the symbolism proper to the actual performance of the sacrament.

The content of the sacramental symbol and sign does not signify the same thing as the celebration of a sacrament. Only if we keep both in mind together, and yet distinct from one another, can we understand completely the manner in which the sacrament signifies and works. What is contained figuratively in the symbolic acts of the sacraments makes a figurative statement about the grace which is administered in the particular sacrament in each case. "The sacraments contain and communicate the grace which they signify."[147] Thus the figurative, symbolic portrayal which takes place in the sacrament is a statement about the grace it contains and which is mediated through it: purificatory washing, edification, the bestowal of office, nourishment. But along with this symbolic statement which is made by the sacrament's content there is yet another symbolism in the sacraments which is perceptible to faith. The sacraments do not merely portray through the content of their signs the grace they effect; they also portray at the same time in the act of their celebration that event through which this grace was attained, namely the sacrificial death of Jesus Christ. And it is for this reason alone that the sacraments have the miraculous power of being able to effect *ex opere operato* the grace portrayed in their signs. The actual *opus operatum* from which grace takes its origin is the sacrifice of our Lord, hidden in the depths of the sacrament which makes it actually present here and now.

We should be able now to observe something similar with regard to the preaching of God's word. It can portray in its content the entire range of God's reality and of his redemptive work for man. But the act of preaching must be distinguished from this all embracing content, and we must inquire whether the fact of preaching itself does not possess a symbolic power of its own. The phenomenon of preaching itself and more especially the hint which the bible gives us by employing the term "word" for Christ make us aware that the act of preaching in the church expresses symbolically that element in the incarnation and life of Christ which complements and supplements that other act expressed in the administration of the sacrament. If the celebration of the sacrament points to Christ's sacrificial death, then the preaching of the sermon points to the climax of God's own sermon, the incarnation of his Son as the word of God to men. In the incarnation God has expressed himself fully and entirely to men. All the words of the Old Testament prophets are a preparation directed to this divine sermon which was preached in the sending of God's Son (Heb 1:1). But after Christ had become man God's sermon in which he summons man could not be finished. For although this was something done by the eternal God who transcends history, he did it by becoming man and by becoming thus a part of history. Hence this event passes away in the stream of history. And after becoming visible to man the word of God passes into the invisible realm of the Father, because this word is at the same time men's answer to God. In fact, the acceptance of this answer by the Father, and therefore the importance of the dialog between God and man, is confirmed by the disappearance of the visible word into the invisible realm through the resurrection and ascension. "And a cloud took him out of their sight" (Acts 1:9).

However it should be possible for all men to participate corporally in the answer given to God by Christ in his sacrifice. All men must therefore be touched corporally by the word which was sent to us, and all must be able to touch corporally the answer which has been made. Somehow or other then it is necessary that not only the sacrifice but also the incarnation, which is the promulgation of God's word, be made continually present in the church. As our Lord's sacrifice, shrouded in the symbolic veil of the sacramental action, is portrayed before men in the church here and now, is it possible for the promulgation of God's word, which found its climax in the incarnation, to be made present, in the veil of preaching, before men in the church. The theologians have repeatedly observed that there is a "profound analogy between the word of God and the sacrament,"[148] though they have always held back from simply equating preaching with the sacraments. "We can compare this event with what happens in the sacrament, though we cannot explain either one. As in baptism a power completely transcending that of nature is imparted through the finger of God to the natural purifying power of water, so God's will imparts a power quite surpassing nature to the natural purifying and vivifying power which can dwell within the word."[149]

Now if such an analogy obtains in any point at all then it is most likely to be in the symbolic signification of word and sacrament. In the efficacy exercised by the two the dissimilarity between them may be greater than their similarity. But in their signification the similarity between the administration of the sacraments and preaching of the word of God may well be greater than their dissimilarity. For what could better proclaim the incarnation of the word not merely in the substance of what it says but by the symbolism of its action than the preaching of God's word through the church's office holders? The spiritual office holder does not then merely portray the incarnate Christ, dwelling among men and preaching about the Father; he also portrays the Father as he sends his Son forth to men. Once he has become man the Son does not of course merely speak of the Father with his words. Rather in becoming man he already is himself the word spoken by the Father to men. The event of the incarnation is portrayed in the event of preaching.

The church makes the rhythm of this dialog visible

through the form in which it celebrates the eucharist with its two parts, the service of the word and the sacrifice. After the service of the word has portrayed symbolically the descent of God's word in the incarnation the sacrifice gives the answer in the sacramental and symbolical portrayal of the sacrificial ascent of Christ in his death, resurrection and ascension, of which the offering of the eucharistic sacrifice is the memorial.

The church's preaching finds its most profound authority not only in the fact that it contains divine revelation. Corresponding to this authority attached to the content of preaching is the special significance given by our Lord to the act of preaching, which is the vessel in which this content is contained. Nor does the authority of preaching lie alone in the fact that those who preach are messengers who are qualified for their task by the sending of the church. This dignity stands in the service of that authority the church's preaching possesses as an image of and participation in, as portrayal and symbol of that first and fundamental sermon God preached to men by sending them his Son. Preaching, so far as it is really carried out as the church's living act, is a saving image and sign of the incarnation of God's son. And this is shown by God's revelation itself. For revelation applies to the incarnate Son a name known to us first of all from the church's preaching. Preaching communicates the word. That is, it transmits what God has communicated in the past, but above all what he has revealed in Christ.

But precisely through the fact that the biblical revelation employs this term which is naturally proper to all preaching to denote God incarnate it shows that the church's sermon is similar to the incarnation. On the basis of what happens in the church's life when the apostles or their helpers preach, the faithful can form quite a clear picture of the incarnation of the Son; for they read that God's word came to us in this incarnation. They know that the apostles and the other messengers of the church proclaim God's word in their preaching. And now it is said to them (Jn 1:1ff; 1 Jn 1:1) that the word of God was from the beginning, that this word was with God, indeed that the word itself is God. They are told that God's word has become flesh so that the apostles could see the word of life with their eyes and touch this word with their hands. Thus the church's preaching must be seen as something similar to the incarnation, as an image of the incarnation. And especially of course because the central object of preaching is Christ, as the apostles' letters in the New Testament clearly testify. But if the church's preaching is at once the proclamation of God's word and the proclamation of Christ, and if, conversely, the incarnation is at once the sending forth of God's Son and the coming of God's word in the flesh, then the similarity of preaching and the incarnation is unmistakbly demonstrated.

That the similarity and kinship of the preaching of the word with the incarnation of the original divine word is not coincidental and superficial, but has been built into the basic elements of the church by the will of its founder and Lord, is shown also by the source from which both have their being. This source is the divine sending: in the case of the incarnation from the Father, in that of the church's pastoral office. It is no coincidence that the chief activity of the apostles in the early church is the preaching of the word of God; nor is it mere chance that these first leaders of the church also bear the title of apostles. Their being sent then is the characteristic fact about these men and their special task. Christ has, in a certain sense, prolonged that sending in virtue of which he comes from the Father in the sending which made his followers apostles instead of disciples, messengers instead of hearers. And the sending which the apostles have received is handed on by them, thus fulfilling Christ's promise to the church that he will be with it until the end of time (Mt 28:20). The church's being sent to preach the word of God is thus in a quite specific sense the continuance of that divine sending through which Christ entered into humanity as the word spoken to us by the Father. In this way the church's preaching of God's word becomes a portrayal and symbolic manifestation of the incarnation of God's Son in Jesus Christ.

3 The Power of Preaching to Impart Grace

What we have discussed hitherto is not significant merely in itself. The fact that the actual preaching of God's word by the church is a symbolic portrayal of the incarnation of the word of God can inspire man to approach this saving event and be caught up in it. But our question is more far-reaching. We ask whether the church's preaching is a sign which actually makes the saving event it portrays so really present before men today that God imparts his grace to man through this preaching. Does man become a co-worker of this saving event when he listens in the proper manner to its proclamation? And does he thus share in the grace this saving event effects?

This is the real question and the discussion of preaching's function as a form of symbolic portrayal was a first step, so to speak, toward answering it. We now find ourselves led from the analogy of the sacraments to the second step.

Our treatment of the symbolic meaning of the preaching of the word was more important since it is only by getting this straight that we can explain the efficacy of the preaching of the word without prejudicing the efficacy of the sacraments as established by the church's magisterium. The reference to the saving event of the incarnation which is set forth in the church's preaching directs our attention to the integration of the preaching of the word with the sacrament in that dual event which is the image of that other twofold event in which our redemption occurred: the incarnation and sacrifice of Jesus Christ.

Christ's Incarnation and Sacrifice as a Single Work

What Christ's incarnation is to the sacrificial death, the preaching of the word in the church's life and work is to the administration of the sacraments. So if we wish to interpret the meaning and significance of the preaching of God's word as something in the church's life whose function it is to mediate grace, then we must direct our attention to the significance of the incarnation for men's redemption and sanctification.

We confess very commonly that Christ's sacrifice on the cross is the source of all graces because it is the meritorious cause of our justification.[150] And in this connection we know too that what Christ has merited was not merely through his death on the cross alone, but through his obedient submission to the Father's will which permeates his entire human life. His whole life stands under the motto which the Epistle to the Hebrews has expressed through an Old Testament quotation (Ps 40 [39]:7–9): "At his entrance into the world Christ says: 'Sacrifice and oblation you did not wish, but you have fitted together a body for me. You took no pleasure in burnt offerings and sin offerings. Then I said: "Here I am; I have come to do your will, O God," as it is written in the roll of the book' " (Heb 10:5–7). His whole life of obedience is summed up in his sacrificial death and laid at the Father's feet. In this way the Father's grace becomes available for us men.

Now the question is what part the event of the incarnation

plays in this occurrence. And just as Christ's sacrifice is not limited to the moment of his death alone, so we must not limit the incarnation to the initial moment of his human existence. The assumption of bodily form by God which takes place in the incarnation continues to take place throughout the whole of Jesus' human life, as through his deeds and words he extends this process of becoming visible and makes it more emphatic.

But what is the relationship of God's incarnation to the sacrifice of the cross, when we ask where the source of grace for men is to be found? Is the incarnation merely the preparation for the sacrifice of the cross which requires this divine and human priest in order that it may be offered? In other words does the incarnation have merely an indirect and mediate significance for our sanctification and redemption, inasmuch as it brings into our historical realm him who effects our redemption in his sacrifice, and in that sacrifice alone? If this be so then it is understandable that people do not suspect in the church's actual preaching of the word, considered as a portrayal of the incarnation, any effective significance for the mediation of grace to men. A one-sided emphasis of the administration of the sacraments as the only source of grace for men corresponds completely with the growing over-emphasis since Anselm of Canterbury of the propitiatory sacrifice as the one and only saving act at the expense of the incarnation.

The Scotist conception of Christ's position has always emphasized that the one-sided emphasis on the propitiatory aspect of Christ's work which necessarily concentrates on the death on the cross alone requires supplementing. And this Scotist view is coming to prevail more and more because of the growing trend toward patristic theology. But the more mystical and physical view which we find in the fathers, and which regards the incarnation as the ontological sanctification of the world, also requires supplementing from the mediatory view of Christ's work laid down in the New Testament, a view moreover which sees his work in terms of a dialog. If the incarnate Christ is God's word to us (Jn 1:1ff; 1 Jn 1:1); if the fullness of time results in God's sending his Son to us (Gal 4:4) and in his speaking to us in this Son instead of in the words of the prophets (Heb 1:1); and if the goodness and loving kindness of the God of redemption are shown in his appearance (Tit 2:11; 3:4); then it is clear that we have before us the conception of a dialog of word and answer in which the divine word must have the initiative without qualification and must therefore receive an emphasis corresponding with this initiative. Even a consideration of the two phenomena of the incarnation and sacrifice makes what holy scripture tells us of these two events understandable. The incarnation is presented as God's descent into our history, the death on the cross together with the resurrection and the ascension as the ascent of the God-man out of our history. And both appear therefore in the mutual relationship of a dialog. We can certainly question the categorical claim that it is "certain that for Paul the 'incarnation' has a redemptive significance only as the indispensable prerequisite for the death of the cross."[152] But even if this claim is true, Paul's major epistles are not the whole of his writings, nor is he the whole New Testament. But if we look at this interpretation of the incarnation as merely the prerequisite for the death of the cross together with the rest of the New Testament, then we must correct the "only" in the above quotation to "also." The incarnation is certainly also the prerequisite which enables Christ to die a death which fulfilled all the demands of propitiation and which was at the same time worthy of God. But that is not all. It is not sufficient, as an interpretation of the incarnation, to say that it is a prerequisite in the sense of something that must exist in order that something else which alone is crucial may occur, but which at the same time remains purely external to this crucial other thing. Rather the incarnation is one part of a twofold total event in which the second part is the answering complement of the first, and in which the first part is also, to be sure, the necessary prerequisite for the second. As in a conversation the word of one of the two partners is the prerequisite for the other's reply, so we can, it is true, call the incarnation the prerequisite for Christ's sacrificial death. But both are essential parts of God's dialog of redemption with men. In this dialog Christ is both word and answer: word insofar as he comes from the Father, answer insofar as he offers his sacrifice for men.

As a work of obedience the death of our Lord is the fulfillment of the Father's word and direction. But this means that Christ's sacrificial death was not something done on his own initiative, but rather the answer which fulfilled something that came from the Father. The sacrificial death appears clearly as the ascending second phase of a total event whose first phase was the descent of the Father's word from on high. Conversely the incarnation is the assumption of flesh by God's word and thus the utterance of this word. The God-man is at the same time the Father's word to us and also the one who is addressed by the Father: he who stands under the Father's command and who answers this command through the obedience of his life up to the point of his sacrificial death. We can say of Christ that he is God's word to us men inasmuch as he came to us from the Father in the incarnation; and he is men's answer to God inasmuch as he ascends in devotion to the Father in his sacrificial death as representative head of the human race. But we can also say of him that he bears the Father's word to us, the word he himself has heard and received as man; and he bears men's answer, spoken first and fundamentally by himself, to the Father on high.

Seen in this light the atonement is not merely the propitiatory sacrifice through which we are redeemed. But it is also not merely the grasping of humanity by God's Son, who descends in order to sum up and to sanctify all things in himself. This is all perfectly true and correct, but it is not everything. We must also keep in mind that this whole process is at the same time a dialog. For the Father speaks his reconciling word to men first in the incarnation of his Son, and this Son then gives men's obedient answer in his life's service and in the sacrifice of his death. The so-called subjective redemption of the individual man means then his participation in this dialog through his reception in faith of the word which comes in the incarnation. This participation is continued when man joins in devotion in offering the sacrifice which is the response to this word. By his participation in this sacrifice man also has a share in the fulfillment of the sacrifice in Christ's resurrection and ascension.

This is the reflection of what our salvation actually is, participation in the life of the triune God. The grace given to us does not allow us to live on as mere creatures before the eternal creator, but makes us in Christ children who stand before their Father. When we receive God's love and respond to it in service and reciprocal love we reflect and participate in what takes place within the triune God in the relationship of the eternal Son before the Father. It is precisely for this reason that that work through which the inner life of the triune God is made available to us and which is the price of this participation has itself the same structure. The word of the Father speaks to us in reconciliation and our answer is borne by the Son in his sacrifice to the Father.

According to this interpretation of Christ's atonement in terms of a dialog, the incarnation does have a real redemptive significance—not for itself alone, but taken together with the sacrifice of the cross. And this sacrifice in its turn does not effect redemption all by itself, but as a partial element taken together with the incarnation. Both constitute together the redemptive dialog in which God and man are a living unity joined in a personal confrontation. The source of the justifying grace of salvation is neither the incarnation nor the death of the cross, each considered alone and in isolation. The source of justification is both the incarnation and the death of the cross, considered as a unity in which each element complements the other.

We must therefore ascribe a causal role in humanity's redemption to the incarnation as well, without infringing upon the causal significance ascribed to Christ's sacrifice on the cross by the official teaching of the church. The sacrifice of the cross always includes the incarnation, as the answer always includes the word. When an answer is effective insofar as it is an answer, then it is the word which has first been spoken that has given it the status of an answer. Thus the answer is effective because, and in the degree in which, the word to which it responds lives on in it. Similarly a statement about the efficacy of the sacrifice of the cross is in reality always at the same time a statement about the efficacy of the incarnation. For the two are related to one another as word and answer. And our statement about the efficacy of the incarnation confirms the efficacy of the sacrifice of the cross. For the incarnation is oriented toward the occurrence of the sacrifice of the cross.

Preaching and Sacrament as a Single Work

The discussion up to this point seems to offer two points of departure which would enable us to take seriously the statements of holy scripture about the efficacy of preaching in imparting grace, while at the same time preserving the function of the sacraments as the effectual source of grace. The two phenomena of the preaching of the word and the administration of the sacraments are a symbolic portrayal of that event in Christ which effects salvation. And like the original reality which they signfy and which is, of course, also a whole composed of two events which are its two elements, these two phenomena are also a unified whole. Now when it is established that one of these elements is, through its symbolic function, necessarily bound up with the imparting of grace, then it is hardly possible to dissolve the unity of these two elements all of a sudden, replacing it with the things existing in single isolation. If that element of this process of symbolism which portrays the sacrifice contains effectually, according to the church's teaching, what it signifies, then we must assume that this fact extends also into that other element of this symbolic process which figuratively portrays the incarnation, namely the preaching of the word of God.

This must not be interpreted however in the sense of a parallelism, as if preaching imparted a grace which comes from the incarnation and the sacrament a grace deriving from the sacrifice of the cross. This would be to tear asunder and isolate what we wanted to see integrated. There is not one grace which has its source in the incarnation, and another with its source in the sacrifice of the cross. On the contrary, all grace comes from a single source. Grace is called the grace of Christ, and that certainly for two reasons: first because grace makes its recipients like the God-man and links them with him in a living unity, but also because it has been caused through the total event of the redemptive work of Christ who descends in the incarnation and who ascends in his sacrifice. The incarnation and the sacrificial death are the integrating parts of a total work which has the character of a dialog. And this work is mediatory because it is performed by the Son of God who is God's reconciling and loving utterance to men on the one hand, and men's devoted, sacrificing, recognizing answer to the Father on the other. The grace given to us is the result of this total process, indeed it is its very image. For in grace God himself enters into the personal inner recesses of man in an image of the incarnation in order to sanctify him. Therefore the fathers of the church and the medieval mystics were fond of conceiving of the imparting of grace to man as a birth of God in the human soul. "From the beginnings of patristic theology people have tried to conceive of the doctrine of sanctifying grace, presented in revelation, in the following terms: the special indwelling of Christ by grace in the hearts of the faithful, who are formed through the church into a single body, is a mystical image and continuation of the eternal birth of the Logos from the Father and of his temporal birth from the Virgin."[153] In this way man is made capable of performing works which are meritorious before God, thus imitating and participating in Christ's sacrifice.[154] These good works which man performs in virtue of his inner sanctification through God dwelling within him are meritorious precisely because they share in what Christ has done on the cross as the meritorious cause of our salvation.

In that case however we shall also have to leave the functions of the church's life in their dual unity in which alone they can portray what has occurred in Christ with its dialogic character of incarnation and sacrifice. Even when preaching and the sacrament are performed apart from one another in time they supplement each other and constitute one single portrayal, as well as a single efficacious cause. The preaching of God's word which is the portrayal of the incarnation does not impart any grace peculiar to itself, just as the sacramental portrayal of Christ's sacrifice does not effect a grace separate from that of the sacrifice itself. But it would be just as incorrect to claim that the preaching of God's word, although it is a portrayal of the incarnation, does not play any part in the effecting of grace, but that it merely prepares for the sacraments considered as the actual cause of grace. To be logical we must say that the ecclesiastical source from which God's grace and justification are imparted to the individual members of the church is the preaching of the word and the administration of the sacraments considered as one single source in double unity.

The isolated consideration of the incarnation and sacrifice of Christ on the one hand and the preaching of the word and the administration of the sacraments on the other hand is no mere theoretical affair without practical danger for a true view of things. This danger becomes quite practical in the question, not infrequently posed, at what moment the church's redemptive activity actually becomes effective. This question seems natural to modern thought with its love of differentiation. It is similar to the question often raised with regard to the doctrine of the eucharistic sacrifice: at what point in the celebration of the eucharist are the Christ who is sacrificed and his sacrifice actually present and portrayed. If a question as precise as this one is raised in this way even within the framework of the portrayal of Christ's sacrifice, then it must arise even more prominently in the dual unity in which incarnation and sacrifice are portrayed. Now it is true that the question is no longer whether preaching as a portrayal of the incarnation or the sacrament as a portrayal of the sacrifice have a causal efficacy for grace. But the same question does appear here in another form. Even if preaching and sacrament are the two component elements of a single process with the character of a dialog they never occur exactly together in time, indeed they are frequently far removed in time from one another. Therefore the precise observer asks at just what point the effect begins to operate. Is the grace produced by the whole process imparted at the moment when the word of preaching is first heard in faith, or only when the whole process has been completed? For preaching is of course only the first phase of this process, and must be supplemented by the administration of the sacrament.

This question is not so easy to answer. But the answer must be that the grace is imparted when the entire process consisting of both phases of that dialog which has taken place in Christ, namely his incarnation and sacrifice, have been portrayed in the church; in other words when preaching and sacrament have actually taken place among and for men. But the question can be raised whether the "when'" in this answer must necessarily be understood in a temporal sense, or whether it cannot also be interpreted in a causal sense. It may be doubted whether a grace of which the mediating cause is the performance of the sacrament and the acceptance of preaching which takes place in the sacrament does in fact exist only after the entire process is complete—not merely in intention and in desire but really and in fact. For we know in other connections that the grace of a sacrament can, under certain circumstances, be received even before the actual reception of the sacrament itself, on the basis of an objective and subjective desire for the sacrament. Now the hearing of the church's preaching in faith is however an objective and, at least in the inclusive sense, a subjective desire for the sacrament, since it is oriented toward the reception of the sacrament. Therefore it could very well be that the grace resulting from this whole process is already given when the actual performance of the second phase is still lacking. To calculate or to reckon how this works out in the individual case goes beyond our possibilities.

At any rate it is established that the grace mediated by the church never comes about solely through the preaching; but neither does it come about through the sacrament alone. It is rather the total effect of preaching and sacrament together. For this grace proceeds from what has happened in Christ, that is, from his incarnation considered as a word, and from his sacrifice considered as the answer, the two partners in this dialog being God and man. But both are portrayed in that single and yet dual process of the preaching of the word and the cult celebration of the sacrament.

CONCLUSION

Where Do We Find Preaching which Effects Grace?

Our considerations throughout this work have been based on the actual life of the church, which truly contains God's word in the vessel of its preaching in order to bring the word's power for grace to men. And yet everything has remained, in a certain sense, still outside the realm of concrete reality. For we have still said continually and more or less hypothetically: wherever God's word is preached with the church's full power it possesses a creative efficacy, inasmuch as it is linked with the church's sacramental cult. That is, God's word communicates not merely knowledge and warning, but divine reality as well. But whether in a given individual case preaching actually possesses this degree of reality or not still remains open to question.

There is a whole host of various ways in which, and occasions when, God's word is proclaimed in the church. We do not say that God's word is proclaimed in all these ways with the same intensity. Actually our entire study presses for an answer to this question as well: where do we find preaching which has the power to impart grace? And if we relegate this question here to a closing consideration as to a sort of appendix, this should not indicate that we consider the question unimportant. The reason is simply that we open up questions here which are still too little investigated. We must be content here with advancing a few considerations which must determine any attempt to answer this question.

Various Kinds of Preaching

Our problem results from the fact that the church's actual preaching of the word of God, which has been promulgated once and for all, takes place not only many times over, but in many different ways as well. And what makes these various kinds of preaching different from one another is a whole host of components which, in ever varying combinations, give form to the church's preaching.

There are three factors above all which determine the nature of the church's preaching and which, taken together, make God's word more or less really present in the church. The first of these factors is the preacher himself, through whose speech and presentation God's word becomes publicly audible in the church. The word of God can be preached in the same outward manner by the ordained holder of a spiritual office in the church or by someone who is not ordained. Furthermore, both the ordained as well as the nonordained preacher can preach in virtue of his being canonically sent or, without the human quality of his word being affected, independent of any such sending, on his own initiative or impelled by the charismatic power of the Holy Spirit. But does the character of the preacher determine the degree in which the word of God he proclaims is really present and really effects grace? Or must we say that God's word remains his word no matter who preaches it?

The second factor we must take into account is the situation in which preaching takes place. The word of God can be proclaimed in a church building in which men have come together to hear it, or in a conference, a lecture, or in school. In the church building preaching can take place in connection with a sacramental service or in a mere preaching service. God's word can be proclaimed in the form of official church teaching by the pope, a council or through the pastoral proclamation of a bishop, or again in the routine instruction in the faith which is carried on under the bishops' supervision. And these different kinds of situation in which preaching takes place also pose the question whether God's word is in every case really present in the same degree.

A further factor which affects God's word as it is preached by men arises neither from the preacher nor from the situation in which he preaches, but from the manner of the preaching itself. This may be considered from a number of viewpoints, but what we mean here is the degree in which human preaching is bound to the written word of God in the bible. *The* permanent form of God's word in the church is holy scripture. Therefore it cannot be indifferent to what degree the preacher allows his own words to be animated by scripture. But to what degree is the power of the church's preaching really to impart grace determined by the extent to which this preaching is animated by the spirit and content of the biblical word?

Proximity to the Sacrament as the Criterion of Efficacy

It is not easy to answer this complex question. It is difficult quite simply because we do not possess any clear official dogmatic guidance in this matter. Nor do we find in holy scripture much unambiguous material to answer the question where the word of God is actually so preached as to be in truth the word of life and reconciliation, the word of grace and of salvation, not merely in the sense of speaking about life, reconciliation, grace and salvation, but so really that, together with the sacrament, preaching actually makes these things to be present in grace. But the question is also difficult because the preaching of God's word is not something which either occurs or does not occur: it can occur of course in various degrees as well. And not every kind of preaching which is not yet preaching in the fullest sense can be said simply to effect nothing at all. Nor does all preaching of God's word which is in truth all that preaching can be attain the very highest degree of potency. Added to these considerations is the fact that the various degrees in which preaching is realized depend upon the various factors we have mentioned, and perhaps upon others as well. Hence it is possible that an act of preaching which is from one point of view a complete realization of what preaching can be may, from another point of view, be less complete.

But perhaps we can after all establish one principle to serve as a guide for an answer to our question. This principle seems to follow logically if the presentation we have attempted is correct in its claim that the preaching of the word and the sacrament are, in the context of their significance, two partial phases of a single process which has the character of a dialog. For it then seems possible to say that the actual preaching of God's word possesses greater efficacy for the imparting of grace the more its connection with the sacrament is not only realized in the sermon, but also visible in it.

Note that what is at issue here is not the intellectual and moral effectiveness through which the word quite naturally influences by warning and by what it communicates. This effectiveness depends on factors different from those that determine the word's effectiveness for grace which we are investigating here. A layman can in a secular framework perhaps, or in personal, private conversation, lead people to the sacrament and thus to grace with an effectiveness which may be missing in the most solemn sermon of an ordained priest preaching within the framework of the church's cult and during the celebration of the eucharist. What is at stake here is rather the genuine efficacy for grace which is peculiar to preaching as a symbolic portrayal of the incarnation of God's word in unity with the sacrament, considered as a portrayal of Christ's sacrificial death. This peculiar efficacy of preaching for grace is probably essentially determined by the degree in which it visibly is what it is intended to be, an act which complements the sacrament in portraying Christ's twofold and yet single work of redemption.

This would then mean for instance that the sermon of a priest who possesses, along with his having been sent by the church, the authorization given to him in the sacrament of orders to portray Christ's sacrifice sacramentally, is closer to the sacrament than the preaching of a layman; and hence, other things being equal, that the priest's sermon possesses greater efficacy for grace than that of the layman. And the priest's sermon probably imparts grace to a greater degree when he preaches within an actual sacramental service than when he does so outside of this framework, for instance in instruction or in a lecture, although these forms of proclamation are also oriented toward the sacraments and are therefore not totally lacking in efficacy for grace. And within the framework of these criteria we must also take into consideration the degree in which preaching is joined to the biblical word. For preaching has received its norm in scripture through Christ's institution, much as the form of the sacramental signs is also determined by the norm instituted by Christ.

"Christian preaching is never purely doctrinal. It has

always a *Sitz im Leben,* a concrete place in life. And this concrete place with which preaching must maintain its contact if it is not to die is divine worship."[155] The preaching of God's word outside of sacramental worship therefore is still oriented toward the liturgical celebration of the sacraments.

If it is true, as Max Picard has written, that "the problem of language begins with the fall, when word and thing were torn asunder," then the healing power of Christ's redemption is also effective here, in the fact that it has, to a great extent, restored to the word its union with the thing. God's self-communication in grace through the word of preaching restores, to a certain extent, that condition of things which Picard imagines as having prevailed before the fall: "When word and thing were still united, when the word did not denote the thing, but was the thing, and when the thing had a name simply by existing, then there was no problem of language. The word was absorbed in the thing and the thing in the word, each was dissolved in the other."[156]

Footnotes

[1] H. Asmussen, *Über die Macht,* Stuttgart 1960, 74.

[2] "The emphasis of the prologue is placed upon the fact that this same son, whose eternal existence before history the evangelist testifies to in the prologue, is he whom the evangelist has seen and touched, the Son of man whom he has to proclaim." J. M. Nielen, "Zur Theologie des Wortes," *Bibel und Leben* 2 (1961), 1–17; this quote taken from 5.

[3] J. Ratzinger, "Christozentrik in der Verkündigung," *Trierer Theologische Zeitschrift* 70 (1961), 4f.

[4] H. de Lavelette S.J. in *Lexikon für Theologie und Kirche* III, 547f.

[5] M. Schmaus, *Die psychologische Trinitätslehre des hl. Augustinus,* Munich 1927, esp. 331–61.

[6] *In Joannem Tract.* 14, 7.

[7] *In Joannem Tract.* 1, 8. See *De Trinitate* XV, 21, 20.

[8] Thomas Aquinas, *Summa Theol.* I, q.37, a. 2 ad 3.

[9] Augustine, *De Magistro* 1, 9.

[10] *De fide et symbolo* 3, 3.

[11] J. Loosen S.J., *Logos und Pneuma im begnadeten Menschen bei Maximus Confessor,* Münster 1941, 42.

[12] Augustine, *De Trinitate* XV, 10, 17.

[13] Denz. 783.

[14] Council of Trent, Vatican Council: Denz. 783 and 1787.

[15] Benedict XII in 1336. Denz. 530.

[16] Denz. 704.

[17] Denz. 1794.

[18] W. Bulst S.J., *Offenbarung: Biblischer und theologischer Begriff,* Düsseldorf 1960, 72.

[19] Denz. 1785.

[20] See J. Fuchs S.J., *Lex naturae,* Düsseldorf 1955.

[21] Thomas Aquinas, *De veritate,* q. 27, a. 4 ad 13.

[22] "This God who alone is true created of his goodness and with almighty power—not in order to increase his blessedness nor in order to strive after perfection, but in order to reveal his perfection through the goods which he communicates to creatures—through a fully free decision . . ." Denz. 1783.

[23] R. Bultmann, "Der Begriff des Wortes Gottes in Neuen Testament,"

Glauben und Verstehen I, [2]Tübingen 1956, 268–93. This quote taken from 273.

[24] Op. cit. 271.

[25] A. Nygren, *Eros und Agape: Gestaltwandlungen der christlichen Liebe* II, Gütersloh 1937, 504f. English translation: *Agape and Eros*, Westminster 1953.

[26] Denz. 1794.

[27] Denz. 842.

[28] R. Asting, "*Die Verkündigung des Wortes Gottes im Urchristentum*, Stuttgart 1939, 66f.

[29] J. Schildenberger O.S.B., "Die Verkündigung des Wortes Gottes im alttestamentlichen Gottesdienst," *Anima* 10 (1955), 296–304; this quote from 302.

[30] See on this point K. Rahner S.J., "Theos im Neuen Testament," *Schriften zur Theologie* I, [3]Einsiedeln 1960, 91–167, esp. 94–96 (English translation: *Theological Investigation* 1, Baltimore 1961, 79–148); see also the same author's *Hörer des Wortes*, Munich 1941.

[31] O. Kuss, "Der theologische Grundgedanke des Hebräerbriefes: zur Deutung des Todes Jesu im Neuen Testament," in *Münchener Theologische Zeitschrift* 7 (1935), 233–71; this quote from 246.

[32] *Mediator Dei, AAS* 37 (1947), 538.

[33] H. Rahner S.J., "Die Gottesgeburt: Die Lehre der Kirchenväter von der Geburt Christi im Herzen der Gläubigen," *Zeitschrift für katholische Theologie* 59 (1935), 333–418.

[34] Denz. 797.

[35] R. Sohm, *Wesen und Ursprung des Katholizismus*, [2]Leipzig-Berlin 1912, 12.

[36] Op. cit. viif.

[37] *Kirche und Verkündigung: Aufsätze zum Kerygma der Gegenwart*, introduced and arranged by H. Burgert and H. Ristow, Berlin 1960, 9.

[38] E. Brunner, *Das Missverständnis der Kirche*, Stuttgart 1951, 13.

[39] Loc. cit.

[40] Y. Congar O. P., "Ecclesia ab Abel," *Abhandlungen über Theologie und Kirche* (*Festschrift für K. Adam*), ed. H. Elfers and F. Hofmann, Düsseldorf 1952, 79–108.

[41] Denz. 695.

[42] J. McKenzie S.J., "The Word of God in the Old Testament," *Theological Studies* 21 (1960), 183–206; this quote from 199f.

[43] Op. cit. 198.

[44] O. Grether, *Name und Wort Gottes im Alten Testament*, Giessen 1934, 127.

[45] Op. cit. 131.

[46] Op. cit. 76.

[47] H. Cazelles in J. Bauer, *Bibeltheologisches Wörterbuch*, Graz 1959, 318.

[48] *Divinum illud, AAS* 29 (1896), 650.

[49] *Mystici Corporis, AAS* 35 (1943), 219.

[50] Denz. 1794.

[51] Loc. cit.

[52] B. Poschmann, "Die innere Struktur des Busssakramentes," *Münchener Theologische Zeitschrift* 1 (1950), 3, 12–30. M. Schmaus, "Reich Gottes und Busssakrament," *Münchener Theologische Zeitschrift* 1 (1950), 1, 20–36. K. Rahner S.J., "Vergessene Wahrheiten über das Busssakrament," *Schriften zur Theologie* II, 143–83 (English translation: *Theological Investigations* 2, Baltimore 1963, 135–174).

[53] K. G. Steck, *Von der Menschwerdung Gottes in Christus,* Munich 1954, 8.

[54] Denz. 40.

[55] Council of Trent, 6th session, introduction: Denz. 792a.

[56] H. Jedin, *Geschichte des Konzils von Trient* II, Freiburg 1957, 59–61. English translation: *History of the Council of Trent,* 2 vol., St. Louis 1957–61. Volume three in preparation.

[57] Summary by J. Beumer S.J., "Das katholische Traditionsprinzip in seiner heute neu erkannten Problematik," *Scholastik* 36 (1961), 217–40.

[58] Denz. 783.

[59] J. R. Geiselmann, "Das Konzil von Trient über das Verhältnis der Heiligen Schrift und der nicht geschriebenen Tradition: Sein Missverständis in der nachtridentinischen Theologie und die Überwindung dieses Missverständnisses," *Die Mündliche Überlieferung,* ed. M. Schmaus, Munich 1957, 123–206. By the same author, "Die Tradition," *Fragen der Theologie heute,* ed. J. Feiner, J. Trütsch, F. Böckle, [3]Einsiedeln 1960, 69–108. By the same author, Schrift-Tradition-Kirche, ein ökumenisches Problem," *Begegnung der Christen (Festschrift für O. Karrer),* ed. M. Roesle and O. Cullmann, [2]Stuttgart and Frankfurt 1960, 131–59.

[60] J. Beumer, S.J., "Das katholische Schriftprinzip in der theologischen Literatur der Scholastik bis zur Reformation," *Scholastik* 16 (1941), 26.

[61] Beumer S.J., op. cit. 27 and 29. See also M.-D. Chenu O.P., *Das Werk des hl. Thomas von Aquin,* Heidelberg-Graz 1960, 263; and by the same author, *La théologie au douxième siècle,* Paris 1957, 329–37. J. de Ghellinck, " 'Pagina' et 'Sacra pagina': Histoire d'un mot et transformation de l'objet primitivement désigné," *Mélanges,* A. Pelzer, Louvain 1947, 23–59.

[62] P. Lengsfeld, *Überlieferung, Tradition und Schrift in der evangelischen und katholischen Theologie der Gegenwart,* Paderborn 1960, 197.

[63] Op. cit. 197.

[64] K. B. Ritter, "Kirche des Wortes und Kirche des Sakramentes," *Die Katholizität der Kirche,* ed. H. Asmussen and W. Stählin, Stuttgart 1957, 86.

[65] A. Köberle, "Wort, Sakrament und Kirche im Luthertum," *Zeitschrift für systematische Theologie* 12 (1935), 273.

[66] "The church is not merely the church of the word (Protestantism) and not merely the church of the sacrament (the danger of the eastern Churches), but at once the church of the word and of the sacrament." M. Schmaus, *Katholische Dogmatik* IV, 1 [5]Munich 1957, 31.

[67] K. Rahner S.J., "Wort und Eucharist," *Schriften zur Theologie* IV, Einsiedeln 1960, 329.

[68] See Council of Florence, Decree for the Armenians: Denz. 695.

[69] Council of Trent, seventh session: Denz. 849.

[70] Origen, *Homily on Leviticus* 1, 1.

[71] See Pius XII, *Mediator Dei, AAS* 39 (1947), 526.

[72] See E. Schick, *Das Evangelium nach Johannes.* Echter-Bibel, *Das Neue Testament,* Würzburg 1956, 71.

[73] *In Joannem Tract.* 6, 7.

[74] This misunderstanding of the author's view is apparently contained in H. Heimerl, *Kirche, Klerus und Laien: Unterscheidungen und Beziehungen,* Wien 1961, 64.

[75] Council of Trent, twenty-second session, ch. 1: Denz. 938f.

[76] "In statu victimae," Pius XII, *Mediator Dei, AAS* 39 (1957), 549.

[77] R. Schnackenburg, "Todes- und Lebensgemeinschaft mit Christus: Neue Studien zu Röm. 6, 1–11," *Münchener Theologische Zeitschrift* 6 (1955), 32–53.

[78] Pius XII, *Mystici Corporis, AAS* 35 (1943), 204.

[79] See Pius XII, *Mediator Dei, AAS* 39 (1947), 551.

[80] Council of Trent, twenty-second session, canon 1: Denz. 948.

[81] Ibid. chapter 1: Denz. 938.

[82] H. Asmussen, *Rom, Wittenberg, Moskau: zur grossen Kirchenpolitik,* Stuttgart 1956, 148f.

[83] O. Dilschneider, *Gegenwart Christi: Grundriss einer Dogmatik der Offenbarung* II, Gütersloh 1948, 257.

[84] See P. Tillich, *Systematische Theologie* I, Stuttgart 1959, 156. English translation: *Systematic Theology* 1, Chicago 1951.

[85] P. Charles, *L'Eglise, sacrement du monde,* Bruges 1960, 158f: "Reflexions sur la Théologie du sermon."

[86] K. Barth, *Dogmatik im Grundriss,* Munich 1947, 98. English translation: *Dogmatics in Outline,* New York 1959.

[87] Denz. 54.

[88] A. Nygren, *Agape and Eros* 1.

[89] *Theologisches Wörterbuch zum Neuen Testament* IV, 133.

[90] R. Asting, *Die Verkündigung des Wortes Gottes im Urchristentum,* Stuttgart 1939, 73.

[91] R. Bultmann, "Der Begriff des Wortes Gottes im Neuen Testament," *Glauben und Verstehen* I, [2]Tübingen 1956, 270.

[92] G. Kittel in *ThWNT* IV, 135.

[93] K. Rahner S. J., "Some Implications of Scholastic Concept of Uncreated Grace," *Theological Investigations* 1, 319–346; see same author in *Lexikon f. Theol. u. Kirche* IV, [2]Freiburg 1960, 994f.

[94] H. Fries, *Glauben—Wissen: Wege zu einer Lösung des Problems,* Berlin 1960, 84. See also A. Brunner, S.J., *Glauben und Erkenntnis,* Munich, 1951; J. Mouroux, *I Believe,* New York 1959; C. Cirne-Lima, *Der Personale Glaube,* Innsbruck 1959, English translation: *Personal Faith,* New York 1965.

[95] K. H. Schelkle, "Das Wort in der Kirche," *Theologische Quartalschrift* 133 (1953), 278–93; this quote from 280f.

[96] Vatican Council, Denz. 1821.

[97] G. Kittel in *ThWNT* IV, 127.

[98] R. Bultmann, "Der Begriff des Wortes," *Gottes im Neuen Testament,* 228, 280.

[99] H. Schlier, *Wort Gottes: Eine neutestamentliche Besinnung,* Würzburg 1958, 17.

[100] R. Bultmann, op. cit. 279f.

[101] R. Asting, op. cit. 133.

[102] K. H. Schelkle, op. cit. 284ff.

[103] *Pontificale Romanum.*

[104] K. H. Schelkle, op. cit. 282; see also H. Schlier, op. cit. 41ff.

[105] Denz. 843a.

[106] Denz. 847.

[107] Z. Alszeghy S.J., "Die Theologie des Wortes Gottes bei den mittelalterlichen Theologen," *Gregorianum* 39 (1958), 685–705; this quote from 686.

[108] Op. cit. 703.

[109] See H. Schlier, "Die Stiftung des Wortes Gottes nach dem Apostel Paulus," *Theologie und Predigt: Ein Tagungsbericht,* ed. O. Wehner and M. Frickel O.S.B., Würzburg 1958, 170–89.

[110] Denz. 844.

[111] M. Schmaus, *Katholische Dogmatik* III, 1; Munich 1948, 797.

[112] Denz. 176, 179; 789.

[113] J. E. Kuhn, "Zur Lehre von dem Worte Gottes und den Sakramenten," *Theologische Quartalschrift* 37 (1855), 1–57.

[114] Ibid. 7.

[115] Ibid. 15.

[116] Ibid. 14.

[117] Ibid. 16.

[118] Council of Trent, Denz. 799.

[119] V. Warnach O.S.B., "'Wort und Sacrament im Aufbau der christlichen Existenz," *Liturgie und Mönchtum, Laacher Hefte* 20, Maria Laach 1957, 68–90.

[120] Ibid. 74.

[121] Ibid. 82.

[122] Ibid. 82f.

[123] E. Haensli S.J., "Verkündigung heute aus lebendigen theologischen Einsichten," *Fragen der Theologie heute,* ed. Feiner, Trütsch, Böckle, [3]Einsiedeln 1960, 463–84. By the same author, "Neueste Versuche einer Theologie der Predigt in kritischer Sicht," *Theologie und Predigt, Ein Tagungsbericht,* ed. O. Wehner and M. Frickel O.S.B., Würzburg 1958, 272–308. By the same author, "Die Krise der Predigt und ihre Überwindung," *Hörer und Predigt, Ein Tagungsbereicht,* ed. O. Wehner and M. Frickel O.S.B., Würzburg 1960, 402–24. The present author's view is not properly represented in this article. J. Betz, "Wort und Sakrament: Versuch einer dogmatischen Verhältnisbestimmung," *Verkündigung und Glaube* (*Festgabe für Fr. X. Arnold*), *ed.* Th. Filthaut and J. A. Jungmann S.J. Freiburg 1958, 76–99.

[124] B. Willems O.P., "Der sakramentale Kirchenbegriff," *Freiburger Zeitschrift für Philosophie und Theologie* 5 (1958), 274–96; this quote from 293.

[125] For a contrary view however see E. Kinder in *Theologische Literaturzeitung* 86 (1961), 283.

[126] K. Rahner S.J., "Wort und Eucharistie," *Schriften* IV, Einsiedeln 1960, 313–55.

[127] H. Schlier, *Wort Gottes* 45.

[128] *Summa theologica* III, q. 60, a.1.

[129] *De veritate* q. 27, a. 4 ad 13.

[130] R. Asting, op. cit. 121.

[131] H. Schlier, *Wort Gottes* 41–3.

[132] *Didache* 4, 1.

[133] Council of Trent, sixth session, ch. 7: Denz. 799.

[134] Ph. Lersch. *Aufbau der Person,* [7]Munich 1956, 381.

[135] Council of Trent, sixth session, ch. 5, Denz. 797.

[136] V. Warnach O.S.B., *Wort und Sakrament im Aufbau der christlichen Existenz* 74.

[137] C. Vagaggini, *Theologie der Liturgie,* Einsiedeln 1959, 422f.

[138] Seventh session, canon 4, On the Sacraments in General: Denz. 847.

[139] M. de la Taille S.J., *Mysterium Fidei,* [3]Paris 1931, 556–78. English translation: *Mystery of Faith,* 2 vol., New York.

[140] Pius XII, Allocution to the International Congress of Philosophers in Rome, November 21, 1946, *AAS* 38 (1946), 428.

[141] Council of Florence, Decree for the Jacobites: Denz. 704.

[142] Denz. 1821.

[143] O. Schoellig, *Die Verwaltung der heiligen Sakramente unter Pastoralen Gesichtspunken,* [3]Freiburg 1946.

[144] Denz. 876.

[145] J. Beumer S.J., "Ein neuer mehrschichtiger Kirchenbegriff," *Trier Theologische Zeitschrift* 65 (1956), 93–102.

[146] *Summa theologica* III, q. 79, a. 2. See also the office for Corpus Christi, antiphon "O sacrum convivium . . ."

[147] Council of Trent, seventh session: Denz. 849.

[148] J. E. Kuhn, op. cit. 19.

[149] K. H. Schelkle, *Das Wort in der Kirche,* 282f.

[150] Council of Trent, sixth session, chapter 7: Denz. 799.

[151] In his work, *Cur Deus homo?*

[152] O. Kuss, op. cit.

[153] H. Rahner S.J., op. cit. 334.

[154] Council of Trent, sixth session, chapter 16 and canon 32: Denz. 809f, 842.

[155] J. Ratzinger, "Christozentrik in der Verkündigung," *Trierer Theologische Zeitschrift* 70 (1961), 6.

[156] M. Picard, *Der Mensch und das Wort,* Zürich-Stuttgart 1955, 35. English translation: *Man and Language,* Chicago 1963.

Biblical References